M000026687

THE UNIVERSAL RULES *of* LIFE

THE
UNIVERSAL
RULES *of* LIFE

**27 SECRETS
FOR MANAGING
TIME, STRESS & PEOPLE**

NABIL FANOUS, M.D.

Forefront
BOOKS

The Universal Rules of Life
27 Secrets for Managing Time, Stress, and People

© 2022 The Canadian Institute of Cosmetic Surgery Inc.

All Rights Reserved.

No part of this book shall be reproduced or transmitted in any form
or by any means, electronic, mechanical, magnetic, and photographic,
including photocopying, recording or by any information storage and
retrieval system, without prior written permission of the publisher.

No patent liability is assumed with respect to the use of the information contained
herein. Although every precaution has been taken in the preparation of this book, the
publisher and author assume no responsibility for errors or omissions. Neither is any
liability assumed for damages resulting from the use of the information contained herein.

Published by Forefront Books.

Cover Design by Bruce Gore, Gore Studio Inc.
Interior Design by Bill Kersey, KerseyGraphics

ISBN: 978-1-63763-023-5 print
ISBN: 978-1-63763-024-2 e-book

This book is dedicated to the memory of my beloved parents,
who taught me, over the years, many of the rules in this book.

Special thanks to my son, Michael John Fanous,
for providing precious insights during the whole writing process.

THE RULES

PREFACE

This book has been in the making for ages.

As a surgeon, teacher, son, husband, and father, I sometimes feel as if I've been studying human psychology my entire life, trying to understand how the world works and how to effectively navigate through it. From the time I was a boy, I was observant and curious about people, and tried to understand what they did and why they did it.

Growing up in Heliopolis, a leafy suburb of Cairo, I attended *Le Collège de la Sainte Famille,* a respected Jesuit Christian institution run by French monks. The Fathers, or *Pères* as we called them, were incredibly erudite. They were well versed in the sciences, literature, and the arts. They worked us hard, from 8 a.m. to 6 p.m. Although they were quite strict with us, we knew that they nonetheless cared for us immensely and were fully committed to our academic and spiritual development.

The Fathers were valuable mentors as well. They spent time with us after school hours, discussing books and poetry, listening to the musical compositions of many European masters, and analyzing German and Italian operas. It was a well-rounded education that instilled in me a love of the arts that lasts to this day.

I was quite fortunate that this wide-ranging educational environment was complemented by a warm and loving atmosphere at home. Both spheres of my early life contributed to the values that fill these pages.

My father, a physician, was a role model. He was easygoing, always wearing a big smile, and seemingly the happiest person on earth. A kindhearted man, he saw the good in everyone and everything. Even when our finances were tight at times, Dad, a devout Christian, donated generously to charities and never worried about money. He exuded faith and optimism. Overall, my father instilled in me a love of life and a reverence for God.

My mother, on the other hand, had a serious and calculating personality. She was blessed with a sharp intelligence and a photographic memory, and had remarkable critical faculties. She exhibited shrewdness and strength, blended with her own brand of love and devotion. Above all, she was filled with profound wisdom about life. Overall, my mother taught me the virtues of hard work and meticulous attention to detail, and she motivated me to excel in any way I could. She coached me on the art of principled thinking, the techniques of effective communication, and the value of moderation in all things.

In order to remain an honor student, I had no choice but to study continually, even on weekends. However, I also wanted to experience some of my father's *joie de vivre* approach: to enjoy reading novels, reciting poetry, listening to music, and communing with nature. I also wanted to indulge my passion for painting and playing squash.

So, with all this to do, I had to figure out how to find the time to accomplish everything. That's when I began looking for ways to more effectively manage my time and the different aspects in my life. And, I guess, that was when this book started to take shape.

I began by reading several works of history, philosophy, biography, and self-help. In essence, when you think about it, all those books were really nothing but opinions based on other people's experiences, including their mistakes and what they learned from them. The lessons these books taught me were infinitely precious to me over the years. Through them, I learned from other people's mistakes. Slowly, I began to see that there are certain ways of behaving, responding and organizing that can make life easier, less stressful, and more enjoyable.

Two of my rules were born.

In addition to reading, I also eagerly reached out to people I respected, including my school mentors and my parents, seeking their advice. And I always took notes diligently (one of my own little secrets in life!), and, most important, reviewed them regularly.

More of my rules followed.

Throughout my life, I tried to act like a sponge, absorbing other people's opinions. I have always believed that everyone I meet has a unique pearl of wisdom to share. I learned enormously from the comments and casual conversations with friends, acquaintances, patients, students, and colleagues. I also had (and still have) a habit of learning valuable information from people I've only met once, such as waiters, taxi drivers, shopkeepers, salespeople, housekeepers, and hotel staff. Even when I heard someone express what first seemed like an outrageous opinion, I always took it seriously and evaluated it, at least for few seconds (another one of my little secrets in life). Some of the most ridiculous notions often turn out to be gems of wisdom in disguise—out-of-the-box inspiration delivered off the cuff.

My list of rules was getting longer.

When I joined McGill University as an associate professor, I taught facial plastic and reconstructive surgery, which showed me how rewarding it is to help restore patients' self-esteem and sometimes, in the process, change lives.

Later, I started to share a small number of these rules with my post-graduate students in the form of an extra-curriculum course. It was an instant success. Students were both entertained and struck by the rules' simple effectiveness. This encouraged me to add more of them to my list. Soon thereafter, I was invited to deliver McGill's Annual James Baxter Lecture, a special event attended by the other professors in my department. The warm response to the first twelve rules, which I incorporated into my talk, encouraged me to start giving presentations about them at various medical conferences.

And as time passed, the rules list kept getting longer and longer still.

Fast-forward to today.

After years of talking about and sharing my rules with students and conference attendees, I finally decided to compile them all into a book.

So, here they are, the 27 Rules—a series of techniques and strategies that will help you feel happier, become more successful, and cultivate better relationships, leading to a greater sense of well-being and peace.

These rules have some amazing benefits:

- You will discover the secrets of how to dissolve procrastination and achieve things now;

- You will learn how to eliminate, delegate, or shrink tasks to streamline your daily life;
- You will master the arts of unitasking and automated living;
- You will understand how to plant the seeds of smart communication and reap the rewards;
- You will discover the transformative power of posture and gaze, and the impact of physical presentation;
- You will unveil some of the secrets to glowing health and longevity;
- You will understand the crucial need to trust your instincts in any social situation;
- You will learn how to ask for what you want, and get it 50% of the time;
- You will discover the power of listening first and talking second;
- You will learn why silence is sometimes your best reply;
- You will see the ways in which gratitude can transform your life;
- You will recognize how living in the moment is one of the most powerful paths to fulfillment.

And a lot more.

In every one of this book's twenty-seven chapters, you will find real-life examples of what to do and what not to do, along with practical prescriptions for managing your time, work, and stress, as well as managing your circle of family, friends, and colleagues. The goal is to help you live a more effective and enjoyable life.

It's all here.

Finally, to this day, I still maintain the habit of learning continuously from my own and other people's mistakes, from the wisdom in books, and from the opinions of anyone and everyone.

*I used this approach over the years, all along my **life**,*
*To find my way in **life**,*
*and to put together my own **life**-guiding principles.*
And slowly, one after the other,
*The Universal Rules of **Life**... came to **life**!*

DO IT NOW, PERFECT IT LATER

Stop the "I Will" Habit

The "I Will" Phenomenon

Every January, millions of people make New Year's resolutions. It's a joyous time full of high hopes.

Ask people what they wish to achieve or hope to accomplish in the following year, and the answer will usually be something such as any of these: "I want to: lose weight; improve my finances; get a new job; exercise more; revamp a relationship; manage stress; stop smoking; set aside more time for myself."

But according to *U.S. News & World Report*, the failure rate for New Year's resolutions is around 80 percent, and most people lose their resolve by mid-February.

Why? Because when it comes time to take action, we hem and haw, deliberate and dither.

We wait for the free time, the perfect day, the right season, a better mood, or optimal market conditions. Or we stall until we can resolve a medical crisis, smooth over a problem with the in-laws, or put some money in the bank.

Rather than adopting a do-it-now attitude, we revert to the "I will" phenomenon: "I will cut out all sweets (beginning next week); I will arrange for us to get together for dinner (really soon); I will pay for gym membership and start exercising (as soon as I get paid); I will put my résumé together (right after the holidays); I will get at least seven hours of sleep (starting next month); I will curtail my obsession with checking my phone (once I've answered all my e-mails)." And on it goes.

There are two major problems with this "I will" pattern.

The first is that intentions and resolutions, which are genuinely expressed in good faith and with vigor and certainty, get us nowhere. *Intentions aren't the same as actions.* Instead, we remain stuck in our comfort zones, avoiding risk and missing opportunities for growth.

The second problem is that whenever the perfect opportunity presents itself, some other hurdle miraculously crops up, and the plan of action is replaced by another "I will" vow. We are easily derailed, seizing any distraction as an excuse to avoid changing our behavior. And the result is failure to achieve our dreams.

> We fail because we never begin!

The Procrastination Racket

Procrastination is a common human handicap, changing our resolutions into broken promises.

Procrastination stops everything. It's a form of paralysis. It's the force that prevents millions of people from getting what they really want, and from bringing their dreams to fruition. It thwarts productivity and hinders enjoyment. And it crushes the possibility for fulfillment. When we procrastinate, our usual rationales for postponement take over, assuaging our guilt and keeping us from advancing our goals.

But why do we procrastinate?

Is it a matter of laziness? It's much easier to delay and wait than to be disciplined and act.

Is it because we're creatures of habit? Habits are addictive and hard to change. We become stuck in our routines, and willpower isn't enough to catapult us out.

Is it because we have an underlying fear of failure? Taking a risk is always a challenge and causes many of us to feel anxious about the unexpected. We dread failure and can't handle rejection.

I would say that procrastination is the result of all three factors. But what can we do to beat it? Is there a neat and easy trick?

Yes, there is.

When Newton's Apple Started Falling . . . and Continued Falling

It was a warm summer night in 1726.

Dr. William Stukeley, an eminent physician, was having dinner with his friend Sir Isaac Newton, the famed English mathematician and physicist. After enjoying a most excellent meal, they both stepped out into the garden to conclude the evening with a fine cup of tea.

Stukeley, in his *Memoirs of Sir Isaac Newton's Life*, published in 1752, recalled that he and Newton were sipping tea under the dappled shade of some apple trees when Newton told him that he "was just in the same situation [when] the notion of gravitation came into his mind. It was occasioned by the fall of an apple, as he sat in contemplative mood. Why should that apple always descend perpendicularly to the ground, thought he to himself."

Triggered by this singular event, Newton, who is recognized as one of the most influential scientists of all time, went on to devise his three laws of motion and set them forth in his *Philosophiae Naturalis Principia Mathematica* (Mathematical Principles of Natural Philosophy), published in 1687.

In his first law, Newton stated what could be simplified as follows:

An object that is at rest—will stay at rest, unless a force acts upon it; and

An object that is in motion—will continue moving, unless a force acts upon it.

This law of physics might as well be a law of human behavior.

It's telling us that:

> **If we do *nothing*,**
> we get *nothing*—and we stay stuck at zero.
> **But as soon as we start *moving*,**
> we continue *moving*—and end up achieving things.

Newton essentially points to us the biggest secret of achievement:

> **Just start taking action . . . and the rest will follow!**

Sir Isaac Newton died in England in 1727, but his famous apple tree continues to grow in the orchard at Woolsthorpe Manor, where he lived.

And every now and then, one of the apples on this tree starts falling . . . then continues falling, and continues reminding us of Newton's first law of motion!

The One Sentence That Made a Bestselling Author

Here is another story.

It's about Glenn Plaskin, an accomplished American author who struggled with procrastination while he was writing his first book.

At the age of twenty-five, he had moved to New York City, armed with a smart idea for what he hoped would become a bestseller. He secured a meeting with multiple editors and, luckily, wound up with a contract.

However, during the first two years of writing what ultimately would become a six-hundred-page biography, he couldn't work effectively. He felt chronically overwhelmed by the task. And he was easily distracted by activities that had nothing to do with writing.

So, one day, as a last resort, he decided to consult a therapist.

As he sat opposite her, he complained that he didn't feel like writing, that he couldn't get into his element.

She stopped him short. "What makes you think I'm interested in your feelings?" she asked.

He was startled, taken aback—insulted, even. *Isn't that why I'm paying you? Why shouldn't you be interested in my feelings?* he thought.

"I'm not interested in what you *feel*," she said with a shrug. "I'm interested in what you *do*."

This was Glenn's *aha* moment. That simple, brilliant statement changed the course of his life. He discovered Newton's first law of motion: *If he just got started, he would gain momentum.*

He didn't need to feel motivated anymore. He just dug into his writing. He didn't attempt to write entire chapters of the book in one sitting; instead, he broke up the material into small chunks and wrote one segment at a time. He didn't dwell on perfecting each paragraph. He just kept going. He felt like he was putting together a jigsaw puzzle. He didn't expect to do it all at once but rather took a piecemeal approach.

In the end, his book became a bestseller, featured in *The New York Times* and *Los Angeles Times*.

His greatest breakthrough, his ultimate takeaway, was to start acting immediately. Yes, it took him three and a half years, but he did it.

So can you.

The "Do-It-Now" Phenomenon

As you might have assumed by this point, the magic formula for mobilizing yourself is to eliminate these two words from your vocabulary: *I will.*

Just do something, anything—as long as you do it now.

It's simpler than you think.

Suppose you keep saying that you will write a letter to a good friend but never seem to find the right time to do it. So, instead of writing the perfect letter, you wind up writing nothing at all. The solution? Just sit down *now* and write a few lines, "I just wanted to say hi" or "How are you doing?" Write something short and simple, then just text it or e-mail it, *now.* It's amazing how easily we can overcome procrastination if we push ourselves to take the first tiny step.

Or suppose there is a book you've wanted to read, but you never managed to find the time to do it. So, just read part of it for five or ten minutes, *now.* The rest of the book can wait for another *now* moment, whenever that comes.

Or if you always seem too tired or too late to go to the gym, try to make it for even ten or fifteen minutes, whenever you have a little *now* opportunity. Even if you end up exercising only fifteen minutes per week, that's still sixty minutes a month. Maybe it's not ideal, but it's definitely better than not doing anything at all, and your health will still benefit from it.

In other words:

Starting—gives you momentum.

As Newton's first law of motion says: *An object in motion stays in motion.* Once you start a task, you're much more likely to finish it. And as Mark Twain said in this famous quotation attributed to him, "The secret of getting ahead is getting started."

So, you don't have to do it all today. Break down intimidating tasks into small, digestible bites. I used the same principle while writing this book. I couldn't do it all at once. I did it one or two pages at a time, whenever a *now* moment presented itself.

Finally, take inspiration from what novelist Nathaniel Hawthorne once observed, "To do nothing is the way to be nothing!"

Perilous Perfection

Taking action immediately has another benefit: it will dampen the urge to act perfectly.

Being perfect is a heavy burden to carry. An obsession with doing the perfect job at the perfect time is a form of self-sabotage that guarantees you will achieve nothing.

Surrender perfectionism.

Even starting awkwardly is still better than not starting at all. Do something now, however imperfect it may be, knowing that you can make it better later.

RULE 1

in a Pearl Shell

Do It Now, Perfect It Later
Stop the "I Will" Habit

- *We Fail Because We Never Begin*
- Do Like Newton's Apple:
  Start Moving . . . and the Rest Will Follow
- *Surrender Perfectionism*
- *Just Do Something, Anything—But Do It Now*
  And Later, You Can Perfect It

UNIVERSAL RULE

2

ASK ONCE
FOR WHAT YOU WANT

And You Will Get It 50% of the Time

The "Too Polite" Phenomenon

You arrive with your spouse at a fancy restaurant for dinner.

The hostess confirms your reservation and asks you to follow her. You do so, and while walking behind her, you notice a nice empty table for two near the window and another one opposite the fireplace.

But the hostess leads you to the back of the restaurant, to the absolute worst table possible—sandwiched between the kitchen doors and the entrance to the restrooms.

One glance at that miserable table and you know you don't want it. Yet, not only do you accept her choice, you even thank her for it!

And for the next two hours, you endure a thoroughly disagreeable atmosphere—the distracting and noisy revolving kitchen doors on your left and the unappetizing customer traffic streaming in and out of the restrooms on your right. It's a nightmare.

But why did you accept that table? Why didn't you ask the hostess for one of the two better tables?

And why did you thank her for following the unspoken rule of many restaurants: save the best tables for demanding customers and offer the least desirable spots to easygoing unknowns?

Why did you keep quiet? Why didn't you assert yourself? Is it because you didn't want to cause a scene? Or you didn't feel entitled? Or you wanted to fit in and please people?

Possibly all these.

The Antidote to "Too Polite"

Let me repeat my question: Why did you remain silent, and even express gratitude, as the hostess led you to the worst table in the restaurant?

I understand that you may not want to act like those obnoxious, pushy, loud restaurant patrons who are looked down upon by decent people such as yourself. However, you don't have to go to the other extreme. You don't have to be the person who is too resigned to argue or too polite to ask—the doormat!

I suggest a simple compromise.

Ask—just once—for what you want.

Whether it's a discount, a favor, a nicer hotel room, a better deal, a more convenient flight, or a date with someone you find attractive, start by asking for what you want—once—even if you think your chances of getting it are slim to none.

You're simply asking a question, and you're only asking once. Those few innocent words might lead you to the desired result.

For example, at the restaurant, you could have simply asked the hostess politely for one of the two good tables you noticed. By just asking once, you're not begging. Neither are you being aggressive. And you won't be stressed about being perceived as too demanding, nor will you chastise yourself later for being too polite.

So, even if you're shy or tend to be a people pleaser, ask once for what you want in life, and there is a good chance that you may get it, or some version of it.

Stevie Wonder didn't *wonder* when he said, "If you don't ask, you don't get."

And as author Peter McWilliams reasoned, "Learn to ask for what you want. *The worst people can do is not give you what you ask for, which is precisely where you were before you asked!*"

You really have nothing to lose!

You may not get all of what you want, but occasionally, you may get some of it. That's still a plus.

Finally, if you have got a little extra courage, you may even go ahead and ask—twice!

However, when you do so, your odds of getting what you want will only go up a little.

The Six Musts of Asking

When you're asking for something, try adhering to the following guidelines:

- *Open with Effective Words Such As "I would like" or "Can I"*
  Starting with "I" in "I would like" or "I would prefer" establishes your assertiveness and keeps the focus on what you want, not on what's wrong with the situation. The second-best starters are "Can I" and "Could you."
- *Keep It Short*
  The longer your sentence, the less persuasive it is, because it may give the impression that you're hesitating.
- *Keep It Realistic*
  Getting what you're asking for will only be possible if your requests are achievable. As Goethe suggested, "If you want a wise answer, ask a reasonable question."
- *Keep Your Demeanor Friendly*
  If you're politely self-assured, it's more likely that the world will give you what you ask for.
- *Maintain Direct Eye Contact*
  This will be further explained in the upcoming Rule 4.
- *And Keep Quiet Once You Have Asked for What You Want*
  Don't say another word. The silence between asking and hearing the answer is crucial. If you keep talking, you will give the other person enough time to formulate an excuse for not complying with your wishes.

The Art of Asking

Asking cleverly is an art form. And like any art, it requires practice.

Following are some suggestions for openers in various situations:

- *If you want a discount:*
  "Could you offer me a better price?"
  "If I buy two, can I have a discount?"
- *If you want a service:*
  "I would like to change the date of my plane ticket" (even if the no-refunds policy is supposedly set in stone).

"We would prefer that table in the corner."

"Can I check out at 4 p.m. instead of 11 a.m.?" (even if the hotel lets you stay only until noon, you're still better off).

• *If you want to socialize:*

"Hi" is still the best, easiest, simplest, shortest, and smartest opener ever—whether at a cocktail party, a professional gathering, or an encounter in an elevator. It's universally well received and almost always receives a friendly response that could lead to an extended conversation.

"How are you?" is second best. And others, such as, "Beautiful day, isn't it?" and "How are things?" are pleasant conversation openers, as opposed to the typical but too-early-to-be-asked questions such as, "Where are you from?" and "What kind of work do you do?"

The "Too Desperate" Phenomenon

As I've explained, asking once for what you want is a practical and valuable approach in most situations, and will get you what you want around 50 percent of the time. That's a good enough percentage for your everyday wants and needs.

But if what you want is of great importance to you, and if your quality of life hugely depends on it, then asking once won't cut it.

For example:

- If you need a loan to save your company from bankruptcy;
- If you want to pursue an intimate relationship with someone who you believe could be the love of your life;
- If you want to place an offer on a home you really adore;
- If you want to have vital surgery performed by the most experienced surgeon in the field, even if he or she is too busy to accept new patients;
- If you want to land your dream job at a competitive company; or
- If you want your siblings to help you to look after a sick parent.

In all such cases, when you're desperate or craving for what you want, and when not getting it would be an unbearable blow to you, then settling for just a 50 percent chance of success is out of the question.

And when the stakes are high, you lose your timidity and pride. The "Too Polite" phenomenon vanishes and is replaced by the "Too Desperate" phenomenon!

Under such circumstances, you don't have a choice but to keep asking. But what do you think would be the maximum number of times you could ask?

Well, I'll let a Colonel give you the answer!

Can't Be a Chicken—When It Comes to Chicken

During the Great Depression, forty-year-old Harland Sanders, owner of a roadside service station, discovered a recipe for fried chicken and started serving some to his customers.

Over the years, he perfected his secret recipe and moved to a more spacious location. Both his reputation and his clientele grew until the day his luck took a turn for the worse: a highway was built through his Kentucky town, and traffic on his road dwindled.

The poor Colonel, as he was called, went broke. He knew he wouldn't be able to survive on his meager pension check. He was desperate and needed a partner, at any cost, with whom he could establish a fried chicken restaurant franchise.

So, he drove his car around for weeks, stopping at various restaurants to look for the right business partner. At night, he would sleep in his car.

He was rejected repeatedly, but he kept asking because he couldn't afford not to get what he wanted.

Finally, he succeeded in finding the ideal restaurateur, one who accepted his proposal.

But how many times do you think Colonel Sanders had to ask for what he wanted? Ten times? Twenty? Thirty? One hundred?

No—a thousand times!

Because for Sanders, it was a matter of life and death. He couldn't take no for an answer.

And from then on, the Colonel's Kentucky Fried Chicken chain went on to become an international enterprise grossing billions of dollars.

What about you? When desperate, how many times could you ask for what you want?

Well, you don't need to figure that one out. The "Too Desperate" Phenomenon will definitely let you know the answer.

It's simple. The more desperate you are, the more times you will end up asking!

RULE 2

in a Pearl Shell

Ask Once for What You Want
And You Will Get It 50% of the Time

- *Don't Be the Doormat!*
- *Ask Once for What You Want*
- Occasionally, *Ask Twice* if Courageous, and a *Thousand Times* if Desperate
- *You Really Have Nothing to Lose!*

START EVERY CRITICISM WITH A COMPLIMENT,

AND EVERY ARGUMENT WITH AN AGREEMENT

How to Criticize and Argue,
Yet Remain Liked and Respected

THE ART OF CRITICIZING

A Scar Is Forever

Nobody likes to be criticized, even if that criticism is constructive.

Haven't we all experienced anger and shame after being rebuked by a parent, a teacher, a spouse, a boss, a colleague, or even one of our own children? In an instant, we are hurt when the antagonist lashes out at us and takes an inventory of our character flaws and misbehaviors. We tend to perceive critical comments as a spiteful and mean-spirited attack. At the very least, they put us on the defensive.

A harsh word can scar us. And like a scar, it can permanently damage us. We remember such comments forever.

> **A criticism is forever.**

That's why mastering the art of constructive criticism is a vital life skill that can benefit you and everyone around you.

A Biased Brain

As humans, we tend to be unappreciative of other people.

We are inclined to undervalue their contributions, zeroing in only on what they're doing wrong. We don't notice their positive qualities, focusing only on their negative ones. We assign fault and blame more often than appreciation and accolades. We are fast to criticize and slow to praise.

Why is that? Because the human brain is wired to react emotionally, rather than logically, to the unsatisfactory things people do. According to research conducted by Duke University professor Scott Huettel, blame and praise are processed in different parts of the brain. Blame is managed by the region that handles emotions, while praise is dealt with in the spot associated with reason.

The result is that people are more likely to assume that positive behaviors are simply accidental, while bad behavior is intentional. This is why we often end up bickering about nothing and finding fault with everything.

For example, how many marriages unravel because of criticism? After years of living with your partner, you find that he or she isn't neat enough, doesn't drive carefully enough, or isn't giving enough. Nothing is enough.

Even if the criticism we offer is on target and constructive, it will just gain us enemies. And it will rarely achieve the result we want.

Striking A Balance

Let's be different from the masses. Let's acknowledge other people's positive qualities and compliment them, before identifying their faults and criticizing them.

If you want to give critical feedback to a colleague, an employee, a family member, or an impressionable child, the best way is to carefully temper your criticism with compliments.

Start every criticism—with a compliment.

On the other hand, don't shower everyone with empty blandishments. It's true that people will initially like you, or even love you, when you deluge them with flattery. But eventually, they will take you and your easy accolades for granted. Your praise will become worthless to them, and you will lose their respect. Worse, you will lose respect for yourself. You can fool people to gain affection, but you can't fool them to gain respect. *To be liked is easy, but to be respected isn't.*

So, try balancing critical commentary with an honest compliment—a genuine one. It's all about striking a balance.

In order to remain a liked and respected spouse, parent, friend, colleague, or boss:

**Be generous with your compliments—
and brief with your criticisms.**

And most important, when you deliver your criticism, use a soft voice and maintain a respectful attitude. It's much easier to swallow a criticism when it's gently delivered.

Penelope's Penalty

Here is a common scenario.

Let's say you're a small business owner. Your assistant, Penelope, has for years done an excellent job of organizing your appointments and running errands.

But lately, things have been slipping through the cracks, and some obvious errors have been made. Most troubling, she forgot to send your tax records to the accounting office on schedule, which has resulted in a hefty penalty for you.

You're quite irritated about it. Your first impulse is to berate her severely for her negligence. But that would be a big mistake. All the goodwill and trust that had been built up over a period of years would instantly become irreparably damaged.

A better strategy is to say, with a tone that's both gentle and firm, "Penelope, do you have a minute? I want you to know that you do an incredible job for me, organizing all the details of our business. I really appreciate it." Then continue, "But lately, it seems as if you might be somewhat distracted. My tax records were not sent in on time, and I'm now faced with a penalty."

By starting with a positive comment and following it with the negative one, you convey the problem loud and clear, but it isn't a personal attack.

It's a balanced, diplomatic approach.

The "Diamond in the Rough"

Have you seen Disney's charming film *Aladdin*?

In the movie, the diabolical grand vizier Jafar, with the support of his sneaky parrot, Iago, seeks a magic lamp hidden in the Cave of Wonders. But the all-powerful Jafar isn't capable of getting it. He doesn't have what it takes.

Only one person does.

He is the modest-looking, seemingly unimpressive street urchin Aladdin. In spite of his drab appearance and laissez-faire demeanor, Aladdin is the only one who possesses the necessary talent for procuring the coveted lamp.

He has *a diamond in the rough*—a talent hidden by a simple and unremarkable outward aspect.

In fact, every one of us has a unique diamond in the rough. It's amazing how many of us beat ourselves up about our flaws and weaknesses and how easy it is for us to discount our own strengths. Our fortes and strong points are often overshadowed in our minds by our foibles and weak points.

The same applies to our perception of other people. It's easy for us to spot their deficiencies but difficult to identify their strengths. To us, their flaws are what's noticeable. That's why your first job is not to be distracted by the obvious flaws and miss the jewel inside.

According to one of my dictums:

> **In every rough, there is a diamond!**

And that applies to you and everyone you meet, no matter how rough the appearance.

So:

> **Look for the *diamond in the rough*.**

Don't just scratch the surface of that rough. Dig deep and pull it to the surface. Search hard for the positive qualities in people and compliment them, before you pounce on their shortcomings and criticize them.

And once you have done that:

> **Expand your compliments—and shrink your criticisms.**

Cut It, Then Close It Please

Teaching surgical residents is a responsibility I take most seriously.

Residents are postgraduate medical students who are nearing the completion of their academic requirements and are eager to take flight. Surgical residents have to struggle through twelve to fifteen years or more of training to perfect their skills as specialists. As you might expect, these are highly intelligent and motivated individuals.

In some medical institutions, the primary focus of education is to teach residents the correct way to deliver medical care and surgical interventions, then closely follow their progress, and inform them of what they do wrong and how to correct it. In other words, it's an approach based on *correcting mistakes*.

But since I started teaching, I decided that my dealings with residents should comprise both *positive and negative feedback*. When I work with residents, as they are learning from me, I am also learning about them. I watch them to detect their strong points and their weak ones, then I highlight the positives before pointing out the negatives.

When I was first offered a professorship at McGill University, I was asked to teach facial plastic surgery to the head and neck surgery residents. In addition to giving many lectures about facial surgery, I also teach multiple extracurricular courses, including one that addresses what I call *The Universal Rules of Surgery.*

This course takes place in a modern university-affiliated facility called the Medical Simulation Centre, where residents often practice on foam mannequins or animal cadavers rather than on real patients, which is obviously not a bad idea! During each section of the course, I demonstrate my surgical techniques, such as how to make a proper incision and how to properly close it, by means of a camera focused on my hands.

Afterward, I ask all the attendees to repeat the procedure at their respective stations. While they are doing so, I make my way from one station to the next to check how everyone is doing.

Again, my goal isn't just to pinpoint what the residents are doing wrong but also to accomplish something more important: *to discover and nurture their hidden special talent—their diamond in the rough.* I look for what they are really good at, what they are gifted with, what comes naturally to them.

For example, I might offer the following constructive criticisms:

"Good job, Dr. A. Your hands are very stable. That's great. I also suggest that when you hold the blade to make an incision, you use three fingers instead of two."

"Your overall posture, Dr. B., while operating, is excellent. It will keep you from having backaches in the future. You also have well-developed hand-eye coordination. Bravo. Now, I suggest you place the ball of your hand over the skin near the incision to better stabilize your operating fingers."

"I like the way you close your wound, Dr. C. Your movements are synchronized, and your stitches are placed in the proper sequence. By the way, rather than holding the forceps far from the tip, try moving your fingers closer to it. This may make it less tiring for your hand muscles."

So, as you can see, my system is to find the students' strong points and reinforce them, before looking for their weak points and correcting them.

Does this system work? It does; the residents really seem to enjoy and appreciate this approach. In fact, I was honored more than once with the Best Teacher Award, which is based on the residents' votes.

However, the biggest gratification for me lies in seeing these young women and men go on to take pride in their work, build successful careers and happy lives, and discover their unique gift: *their diamond in the rough!*

THE ART OF ARGUING

Bridges: Built or Burned?

The usual form of arguing—back and forth, with a complaining partner, a frustrated client, or an aggressive boss—is a total waste of time. And it's a recipe for disappointment on both sides.

When we argue, our emotional buttons are pushed and our tempers flare. And as we become more emotional, rational thinking flies out the window. Escalating arguments between individuals only cultivate an atmosphere of hostility. In the end, such conflicts typically burn bridges rather than build them. It's like lighting a spark and watching a fire spread.

That's why:

> **It isn't a good idea to start an *argument* by . . . *arguing!***

Here is a far superior, if counterintuitive, approach that really works:

> **Start every argument—with an agreement.**
> **If you have to argue, start by agreeing . . . on something!**

This will initiate an amicable dynamic and make the other person more receptive to your point of view.

You let the opponent score first . . . which will make him or her more willing to let you score second.

However, if there is nothing you can agree on, just say:

> **"I understand what you mean."**

By doing so, you're confirming that you have heard what the other person is trying to convey, without necessarily agreeing or disagreeing with it!

Two Girls in the Morning

A few years ago, Denise, a famous TV talk-show host in Montreal, Canada, came to see me for a consultation regarding a facelift. She was an attractive woman in her forties with a forceful, charismatic personality.

During our conversation, she confided in me that she had already spoken with three other plastic surgeons before coming to see me. She explained that she would make her final decision after her visit with me.

In addition, she told me that she was planning to make a documentary about her facelift experience. It would be broadcast on her very popular French Canadian television show *Deux filles le matin* (Two girls in the morning).

As she explained to me, whichever surgeon she chose would benefit from extensive media exposure, though that surgeon would also come under the scrutiny of a national audience—the result of her facelift would be inspected and judged by hundreds of thousands of viewers.

As I examined Denise, I suggested that she undergo a combination of two of my minimally invasive techniques: a mini facelift (lifting the face with minimal surgery and precise sutures) and a mini forehead lift (lifting the brows a little bit with very small hidden incisions).

Denise's reaction was swift, expressed in a rather dry tone. "The other three plastic surgeons suggested that I get a full facelift and a simple eyelid lift. And none of them said anything about my forehead," she said.

I knew that arguing about the merits of my approach would be unproductive. So, I began my reply with an agreement, a genuine one.

"Denise, I fully agree with the other three surgeons that having an eyelid lift is simpler and will make you look younger. And I totally respect their opinions." Then I paused.

"Why wouldn't you do it, then?" she asked with a perplexed expression.

"Because in every surgery, there is more than one acceptable technique for any given condition. Different good surgeons may offer different good opinions," I replied. "It's true that the eyelid surgery will make you look younger, but it has one drawback in your case."

"What's that?" she asked, appearing more curious.

"In my opinion, although eyelid surgery is a very good technique in general, it's not the ideal one for you. It's true that you would look younger once the excess skin of your upper lids is removed, but you may look a little sadder too," I replied.

"What! Sadder?" she exclaimed.

"Yes," I resumed, "because your brows are now somewhat low and may become a touch lower after that surgery. The problem with low brows is that they impart a tired and sad look. However, with the mini forehead lift that I am proposing, I could move your brows up by just two or three millimeters, using only three tiny incisions of two centimeters each, which would be concealed in your scalp. I would even be able to do that without shaving any of your hair and without any incisions on the lids. You will gain a younger and more open look, and your facial expression will be a fresher and more alert one."

I then handed her a mirror and proceeded to move her brows a few millimeters up with my hands in order to give her an approximate preview of her result.

Denise seemed fully engaged in my demonstration. Then, looking thoughtful and somewhat troubled, she murmured that she understood my point of view and would think about it.

Two days later, Denise called the clinic and booked her surgery. The procedure went perfectly, and Denise was totally pleased with her refreshed and younger but still natural looks.

Two months later, Denise was on TV for a full hour, describing her ultimately happy experience, showing her results, and occasionally mentioning my name!

The episode was a big hit and proved to be one of the most popular in the history of the show. Over the following few months, our phones didn't stop ringing.

And all because before I argued . . . I agreed!

RULE 3

in a Pearl Shell

Start Every Criticism with a Compliment, and Every Argument with an Agreement
How to Criticize and Argue, Yet Remain Liked and Respected

Criticizing
- *A Criticism Is Forever*
- We Are Fast to Criticize, and Slow to Praise
- *Start Every Criticism with a Compliment*
- Be *Generous* with Your Compliments, *Brief* with Your Criticisms
- *In Every Rough, There Is a Diamond*
  Look for the *Diamond in the Rough*

Arguing
- *Don't Start an Argument by ... Arguing!*
- *Start Every Argument with an Agreement*
- Let Your Opponent *Score First*, So That You Can *Score Second*
- If You Can't Agree on Something, Just Say,
  "I Understand What You Mean"

STAND STRAIGHT, LOOK STRAIGHT

*How Your Posture and Gaze Can Create
a Commanding Presence...
Before You Even Utter a Word*

The Seven-Second Myth

The moment a stranger sees you, his or her brain makes a thousand computations.

Do you have status and authority?

Are you trustworthy, competent and confident?

Are you someone to greet or avoid? A possible friend or foe?

These judgments are made at lightning speed. In fact, according to articles in *Business Insider* and *Forbes,* the general consensus among experts is that first impressions are crystallized within seven seconds. And these impressions lead to major decisions that may spell the difference between a positive and a negative interaction.

However, newer evidence suggests that first impressions may be formed in even less than seven seconds. Is it six? Five? Four? Maybe even three seconds?

No, none of these!

The department of psychology at Princeton University has been one of the most revered in the country for more than a century.

In a landmark research study involving 245 undergraduate students, one of its eminent former professors, Dr. Alexander Todorov, conducted five experiments, each focusing on the amount of time it takes, in seconds, to form a first impression and judge various traits such as competence and attractiveness.

The result of his study was mind-boggling. Its conclusion:

First impressions form within ... one-tenth of a second!

Interestingly, Dr. Todorov also found that these snap judgments didn't significantly change, even when additional time was given to the participants in the study.

Therefore, when meeting strangers, and before you even open your mouth, you almost instantly telegraph a message, a memo, a kind of miniature CV about who you are and how you feel about yourself.

So, whether you're in an interview, on a date, or in a meeting with a new client, it's important to be aware of the way your presence is perceived, and the way you influence the opinions of others. Indeed, the clock is ticking. And you only have a fraction of a second to make a lasting impression.

> **You have got one-tenth-of-a-*second* chance . . .**
> **and you'll never get a *second* chance!**

A Royal Handicap

People make instantaneous and unconscious judgments about you when they first spot you from afar, long before they ever come close to you physically.

You might say that your body language is your calling card, rapidly revealing where you fall on the personal confidence scale. That's why your posture and gaze matter greatly when it comes to first impressions.

> **A confident posture and a focused gaze—**
> **are your telltale signs of self-assurance.**

Proper posture and a focused gaze show the world that you're sure of yourself, competent, and worthy of trust and attention. They convey the impression that you know where you're going and what you're doing.

What do you suppose you would convey with a hunched back, sagging shoulders, and an unsteady walk? This kind of body language transmits weakness, lethargy, and a defeated spirit. It's as if you're weighed down by gravity, as if you're carrying the Himalayas on your shoulders.

Rather, to make a positive first impression, hold your head high, pull your shoulders back, and keep your spine aligned, all while being relaxed—without being stiff.

Similarly, a distracted, unsteady, or unfocused gaze sends nonverbal cues of insecurity, shyness, and uncertainty. Why, then, should anyone take notice of you, acknowledge your presence, or pay attention to you?

Rather, keep your gaze direct to greatly enhance your initial impact. The bottom line is:

A slumped posture and poor eye focus—
are the King and Queen of bad first impressions!

If this applies to you, then you will need to abdicate immediately, Your Majesty! And off that wobbly throne thou must go.

And you will need to work fast and hard on applying the magic recipe for instant status and enduring presence—the concoction of confident posture and focused gaze.

Your Confident Posture

It all starts in childhood.

How often did your parents tell you to stand up straight? They knew that a confident posture could have a positive effect on your future. Yet, as adults, we still don't make the effort to improve our posture.

A confident posture is:

Standing tall—and walking tall.

And it has many benefits:
- *A Confident Posture Projects "Power"*
  If you're bent over while you walk, you look bedraggled, sloppy and haphazard. It's as if you're being pulled by marionette strings, with head, arms, and legs swinging and flailing in all directions. This conveys powerlessness, insecurity, and mediocrity. It's the antithesis of power and self-assurance.

But when you assume a confident pose, your brain gets a signal that the confident you is in charge. By adopting a confident stance, you actually feel more powerful.

• *A Confident Posture Projects "Success"*

Standing tall bestows on us an aura of prosperity, a nonverbal signal of accomplishment. "Success isn't everything, but it makes a man stand straight," noted dramatist Lillian Hellman.

• *A Confident Posture Enhances "Health"*

The late Dr. Rene Cailliet, a musculoskeletal researcher, reported that slouching decreases lung capacity, reducing the amount of oxygen in your body. But when you open your chest by letting your shoulders go back and lifting your head, your lung function is enhanced.

Another study performed at Ohio State University showed that keeping an upright posture lowers your stress level.

In addition, a confident posture can have an impact on your mind. Researchers at Harvard and Columbia Universities have studied the link between bad posture and the brain for decades, and their findings show that better posture can improve the brain's performance both in terms of mood and memory levels.

• *A Confident Posture Enhances "Safety"*

Ephrat Livni, an American writer, reported a study in which psychologists asked convicted criminals to watch videos of pedestrians walking down a busy New York City sidewalk and pick out potential victims. The hunched and slumped individuals, predictably, appealed to the criminals the most.

Posture, more than a person's size or apparent strength, was a key factor in their choice.

• *A Confident Posture Enhances a "Youthful Appearance"*

"The most important thing is posture. When you get old, it's the way you walk and the way you stand that shows it," former fashion model Carine Roitfeld noted.

The Six Musts of Confident Posture

A compelling posture has six fundamental components.

• *A High Head, a Straight Neck, and a Level Chin*

All maintained in a relaxed rather than a stiff manner.

• *A Well-Aligned Upper Body*

It all starts with the position of your spine, which has three natural soft curves—at your neck, in the middle of your back, and at your lower back. A confident posture should maintain these curves, not increase them. Your head should be centered above your shoulders, and the tops of your shoulders should be positioned over your hips.

• *Softly Swinging Arms*

While you're walking, as one foot steps forward, the opposite arm swings forward too, as a natural balancing act. In other words, the right foot and left arm move together, followed by the left foot and the right arm.

Make sure your arm movements are relaxed, as if you have a weight dangling by a thread from each shoulder.

• *A Heel-to-Toe Gait*

Each step should begin at the heel, with the foot imprinting progressively along the sole to the toes.

• *A Balanced Stance*

When you're standing, both feet should be planted on the ground. Shifting your weight from leg to leg makes you look fidgety.

• *An Expansive Width*

A Northwestern University study discovered that positioning yourself in a way that opens up the body and takes up space activates a sense of power. As psychologist Amy Cuddy explains, "In the animal kingdom, power and dominance is about expanding: making yourself look bigger."

So, take up more space when you sit or stand!

Your Focused Gaze

While you're walking or talking, if you're looking down, blinking or moving your eyes, it subliminally conveys insecurity, irrelevance and lack of trustworthiness. However, a proper focused gaze creates an instant aura of confidence.

A focused gaze means:

> **Looking straight ahead—while walking,**
> **and looking directly at the other person—while talking.**

Stop the evasive eyes habit, whether you're walking or talking. Give people the respect of your full gaze rather than habitually looking across the room, at the ceiling, at the floor, or at your phone, all of which can indicate distraction and lack of interest.

The Three Musts of a Focused Gaze

As explained, a compelling gaze is simply a matter of focused and fixed visual engagement.

Such a gaze has three fundamental components:
- Looking *Straight* Ahead
- Looking *Where* You're Going
- Looking *at Whomever* You're Talking To, Without Staring

To avoid staring, writer Carol Kinsey Goman suggested an interesting trick: "When facing someone, try to find out the color of his or her eyes!"

RULE 4

in a Pearl Shell

Stand Straight, Look Straight
How Your Posture and Gaze
Can Create a Commanding Presence . . .
Before You Even Utter a Word

- *Slumped Posture and Poor Eye Focus*—Are the *King and Queen* of Bad First Impressions
- *Confident Posture and Focused Gaze*—Are the Recipe for a Commanding First Impression
- You Have Got *One-Tenth-of-A-Second Chance . . .* And You Will Never Get *a Second* Chance!

LISTEN FIRST, TALK SECOND

How to Mesmerize Anyone You Talk To

Darwin's Dud

If two people are having a conversation, one person is talking while the other is listening. Or so you think.

In today's high tech, high-speed world, the faculty of listening has evolved—in the wrong direction. It has undergone an unorthodox path of evolution that Charles Darwin, author of the theory of evolution by natural selection, failed big-time to foresee.

The art of listening has almost become extinct. When people aren't talking, their ears are tuned out and their minds are somewhere else. We are driven to distraction, our minds on overload, consumed only with our own needs and thoughts.

You might be talking to someone about your view of the stock market or a traffic jam, while he is thinking about the movie he saw last night or when he can replace his car tires. Your words simply go in one ear and out the other. Yet that person is looking straight at you, pretending to be listening!

There is another version of not listening too—it involves people who constantly interrupt you, talk over you, or belittle you. For example, say you're conversing with a friend and, right as you begin to talk, that person cuts you off, disagreeing with your very first incomplete sentence, then plunges into an unstoppable tirade to prove his or her point of view, without ever giving you a chance to state yours. It's downright rude and yet so commonplace.

Reviving the Art of Listening

Now, what can you do to bring back the art of listening?

You obviously must avoid both fake listening and interruption. "We have two ears and one tongue so that we would listen more and talk less," suggested the Greek philosopher Diogenes.

So:

Listen first, talk second.

In fact, people are so accustomed to not being listened to that they will feel embraced and supported by anyone who actually does listen to them.

A good listener is a rarity. Train yourself to be such a rare active listener. Whether talking to staff, clients, friends, or loved ones, *focus on what's being said* rather than whatever else is going on in your mind.

And as you know by now, do this by maintaining *eye contact* and an *attentive posture*.

Giving other people the opportunity to express themselves fully, with no interruption, and allowing them to take center stage and bask in the spotlight, is a passport to success.

In doing so, you will acquire valuable social currency in a talk-first, never-listen culture.

Charming Charles

After being inaugurated as the youngest president of the United States, John F. Kennedy needed to make an important decision: which foreign country to visit first, England or France?

The stakes were high. Kennedy had important political goals to achieve in both countries, and he needed to win their leaders' goodwill and friendship. England was the closest ally to the United States during World War II and was the obvious, expected choice.

Yet Kennedy chose France instead. Why? Because France had Charles de Gaulle as president. And de Gaulle was known to be an imposing presence and the hardest-to-impress figure among world leaders.

So, on May 31, 1961, President and Mrs. Kennedy undertook their first transatlantic state visit. As they landed in Paris, they were greeted by Le Général himself.

De Gaulle was a formidable gentleman at six feet five inches tall. He was stubborn, willful, and a supremely self-confident leader with an enormous ego. More than his towering height, though, it was his resolute bearing and his imposing posture that gave him an air of great authority and charisma (*Stand Straight, Rule 4*).

In his book *Leaders*, President Richard Nixon wrote that de Gaulle "seemed to tower over the rest in dignity and stature, as well as in height, and displayed an enormous, even stately dignity." Nixon added, "An aura of majesty seemed to envelop him. In the grandeur of Versailles palace, de Gaulle looked completely at home."

Interestingly, it was at another grand palace, L'Élysée, that the Kennedys enjoyed their welcoming state dinner. First Lady Jacqueline was seated next to de Gaulle, who was reputed to be aloof and averse to indulging in small talk.

But guess what? De Gaulle spoke extensively to the first lady. In his book *Jacqueline Bouvier Kennedy Onassis: A Life*, Donald Spoto said that at one point de Gaulle turned to President Kennedy and said, "Your wife knows more French history than any Frenchwoman." He then turned back to Jackie and did not take his eyes off her for the rest of the meal.

What happened? It was Jackie who made the difference. The first lady was renowned as an exceptional listener. She had a reputation for engaging politicians and celebrities with her keen ability to focus on a speaker and respond wittily with remarks that invited a good rapport. She would look people in the eyes, listen intently to them, hang on to their every word, and make them feel important. In addition to all that, she spoke French!

Le Général was dazzled. Jackie, a charming listener, won the heart of President Charles de Gaulle, a man who was bigger than life and not easily beguiled.

As psychologist Karl Menninger declared:

"Listening is a magnetic force."

Indeed.

The Concerto Conversation

A *concerto* is a musical composition that highlights *a solo instrument* against the background of *a full orchestra*.

For example, the soloist (say, a pianist or a violinist) takes the lead in an interplay with the other orchestral instruments. It's an enchanting musical dialogue, almost like a human conversation, in which the solo instrument is the main speaker, dominating the performance.

In other words, the solo instrument *talks,* and the orchestra occasionally *replies.*

Good listening, like playing a concerto, is all about timing.

When someone talks to you, that person is like a solo instrumentalist and should therefore be the center of attention. And you, like the orchestra, should perform a supporting role, chiming in when appropriate, knowing when to remain silent.

So:

**Listen intensely to others (the solos),
and talk only when necessary (like the rest of the orchestra)!**

It's a simple but rare skill that has immense benefits. It endears you to the people you converse with because it conveys a genuine interest in what they've got to say.

Also, by truly listening, you not only provide a willing ear, support, and kindness, you also may wind up being enriched by something you hear.

The Unheard and the Unseen

You probably remember growing up and listening to your parents' conversations.

It wasn't just *what* they said, but *how* they said it and how they *looked* when they said it, that enabled you to figure out what they meant. With just a phrase, you knew immediately where the conversation was headed. You could tell if you were going to be rewarded or rebuked.

Today, as an adult, you also have the opportunity to analyze conversations: the speakers' tones of voice and verbal subliminal messages all transmit valuable information about the meaning of the words you're hearing and the speaker's personality, intentions and needs.

As author Nina Malkin observes, "The best listeners listen between the lines."

Even in business, by listening astutely to what is and isn't said, you will be better able to maneuver, strategize, negotiate, and clinch deals. And this promotes reciprocally profitable relationships.

So:

Focus on what you're hearing—but not hearing!

Try to figure out what the other person isn't saying. "The most important thing in communication is hearing what isn't said," noted the late management guru Peter Drucker.

As well, ask yourself, *What should I see, but am not?*

So:

Focus on what you're seeing—but not seeing!

Note the speaker's facial expressions, posture, and eye movements, all of which reveal aspects of his or her motivations.

When you're talking to people, think of what they're saying as a message projected on a movie screen, communicating information about them both aurally and visually. You can decode that information by listening and watching diligently.

RULE 5

in a Pearl Shell

Listen First, Talk Second
How to Mesmerize Anyone You Talk To

- *Listening Is a Magnetic Force*
- Start by *Listening* before You Start *Talking*
- When You Listen, *Listen with Your Ears and Eyes*
  Hear What's Not Said, and *See* What's Not Seen!
- And Before You Talk, *Wait—Like the Rest of the Orchestra!*

ELIMINATE IT, DELEGATE IT, OR SHRINK IT!

*The Three Time-Management Secrets of Doing...
What You Don't Have Time to Do*

> ## THE FIRST SECRET OF TIME MANAGEMENT
> The best way to do something *that doesn't need to be done* . . .
> *is not to do it at all!*
> In other words: ***Eliminate it.***

Eliminating the Unnecessary

It's only logical. If you put too much weight on a mule, the poor thing won't be able to move. Neither could you.

But how many of us attempt to accomplish everything and relentlessly pile it on, overloading and stressing ourselves?

There are a variety of tasks and time-wasting activities—*which don't have to be done at all*—that are weighing you down. Ask yourself what would happen if you eliminated these unnecessary tasks.

Would your world fall apart? Of course not.

Elimination Target 1: Phone, E-mails, and Social Media

For most people, checking their cell phones is a perpetual temptation, a compulsive urge. Our phones are like our security blankets. We are incapable of leaving home without them.

According to a study conducted by Asurion, a phone insurance and support company, Americans check their phones every ten minutes, on average. That's nearly one hundred times per day.

Why so much phone checking? *Because we feel as if we're going to miss out on something.* We're dying to keep up with what's happening. This fear of missing out has become so prominent that it even has its own acronym—FOMO.

But this constant checking jeopardizes our quality of life and drains our ability to be productive and feel calm and happy. Repeatedly looking at texts, e-mails, and social media feeds causes continual distraction, which steers us away from our other responsibilities and interferes with our personal relationships. The result: face-to-face communications are abbreviated and social skills are waning.

So:

Eliminate habitual phone checking.

However, the only way to evict such a bad habit is to replace it with a good one.

Here is an approach that will simplify your digital life.

The Seven Smart Formulas

There are seven effective formulas that will help you keep your checking-in addiction . . . in check:

- *The Time-Windows Formula*

  Limit your phone usage to three windows of 10 to 15 minutes each day. These time slots could be scheduled, say, first thing in the morning, during your lunch break, and at the end of the day.

  Use them to scan your e-mails and notifications, read your texts, sift quickly through your social media feeds, and reply to any of these if necessary.

- *The One-Minute Formula*

  A minute is a long time—if you know how to use it. One minute or less is often what it takes to respond to a text message or an e-mail.

  The secret is to be brief. Shave off the fat and go straight to the meat of the matter. Use crisp, short, to-the-point sentences, as well as clipped openings and closings. For example, a typical e-mail might go something like this:

  Dear John,

  Thanks for sending me the car insurance estimate. I am fine with all the clauses except number 4, the one about the $3,000 deductible. I find it too high. Is it possible to lower it to $2,500? Please let me know.

  Best regards, Michael.

  The following is the one-minute alternative:

  Hi, John, I agree except for clause 4. How about $2,500 instead of $3,000? Thanks, M.

  Got the idea?

- *The Silenced Notifications Formula*

Sounds and vibrations from your phone are a major distraction and an annoyance to everyone around you. Turn off your notifications except for a select few, such as calendar reminders, phone calls, text messages, and e-mails from your primary e-mail account.

All others should arrive silently and can be screened later during your time windows.

- *The Ringing Phone*

When you hear your phone ringing, remember this: *It's a phone ring, not a command!*

Think before you pick it up. If you're busy or not in the mood, you don't have to answer, unless you suspect the call is urgent.

So, resist the habit of automatically answering a ringing phone. And by doing so, it will discourage calls from colleagues and acquaintances who are looking for instant gratification by chitchatting on the phone whenever they are bored.

- *The Block/Unsubscribe Formula*

Block bothersome callers once, and they are gone forever. As well, block or unsubscribe from undesirable e-mails addresses.

As for unwanted e-mails that you can't block for whatever reason, just send a reply announcing that your e-mail address has been changed to a new one (an inactive one! as you'll see later).

- *The Social Media/Apps Formula*

Turn off social media except two or three that are essential to connect with family and friends. And delete all non-pertinent apps that suck up your time and attention, especially games.

- *The CC/Reply All Formula*

When you reply to group e-mails, resist using both the *CC* line and the *Reply All* button. This will eliminate unnecessary e-mail replies in the future.

Finally, tablets and laptops are nothing but magnified versions of your phone. Therefore, all the preceding formulas apply to them.

Elimination Target 2: Unnecessary E-mail Accounts

Eliminate all your e-mail accounts except three—two active and one inactive.

Your active e-mail accounts should be the ones that you use and check regularly: one personal, for friends and family, and the other professional for work and business contacts. If you own your own business, you can add an e-mail account dedicated solely to billing, ordering, and customer service inquiries.

Your inactive e-mail account, on the other hand, is the dormant one that you will never ever check. It's the one to give to merchants and advertisers whom you don't ever want to hear from!

Elimination Target 3: Television and Subscriptions

According to statistics (that constantly vary with years and between age groups), Americans seem to watch television for an average of around three to five hours per day, in addition to about the two to four hours spent checking other screens—smartphones, laptops, and tablets—each day.

This is physically unhealthful. Watching too much television or too many videos turns us into couch potatoes. In addition, excessive screen time can cripple our social skills. Instead of isolating ourselves in front of a screen, we should be around people who energize us and make us happy.

It's time to create boundaries around our TV viewing habits. Personally, I try to limit myself to half an hour of TV per day, plus three fifteen-minute smartphone-checking windows.

The same concept applies to publications—whether print or digital. If you subscribe to too many of them, you will rarely get a chance to go through any of them. The only sure thing you'll achieve is stress and guilt every time you see those piles waiting for you.

So, cancel digital and print subscriptions to everything except the one or two magazines or journals that are most interesting to you.

> ## THE SECOND SECRET OF TIME MANAGEMENT
> The best way to do something *you don't have to do personally* . . .
> *is to let someone else do it for you!*
> In other words: ***Delegate it.***

The "Doing Everything" Phenomenon

Don't be guilty of one of the major sins of time management: attempting to do everything yourself.

If you have a full-time career, why do you also need to clean, organize, file, shop for groceries, mow the lawn, and bathe the dog? Rather, you should learn how to delegate.

When you delegate, you shouldn't be moving *the tasks that only you can do onto somebody else's plate.*

Instead, delegation means getting *the tasks that you don't have to do yourself off your plate.*

It's important to understand the difference.

For example, perhaps you can pass some of your tasks to a young neighbor, a student, a friend, one of your children, or a retired relative. In addition, you can hire outside helpers and virtual assistants to help you with almost anything you need. Instant assistance is at your fingertips via the ever-increasing number of internet service companies, often with little cost to you.

The Before and After of Delegating

Whenever you delegate, you must first explain how you want the job done.

Invest time—once—into teaching your chosen helper how to do the task properly, then assume that the lesson has been learned.

However, your responsibility isn't over once you've delegated. You still have to repeatedly check the work of the people you've assigned the tasks to, not only to make sure the tasks have been done, but also to make sure they've been done well.

Supervising the work of others takes very little time, but has to be done regularly. Why? Because if the people you're delegating to realize that you're not checking on them, sooner or later they might start cutting corners, or even skip doing the task altogether.

So:

Delegate and teach—
then check and recheck.

Finally, once you have delegated, trained, and set up a schedule for checking in, back away from the task.

Don't micromanage. You have to let go between checkups.

THE THIRD SECRET OF TIME MANAGEMENT
If you can't eliminate it and can't delegate it . . .
then at least **shrink it!**

How to Shrink Tasks

Most tasks can be minimized by simply skipping some portion of them.

For example:

If you're invited to a social event, skip the beginning by arriving late, or arrive on time but leave early.

If you're organizing an office meeting, skip the introductions and the least-relevant points of discussion.

If you're writing a letter, a text, or an e-mail, skip the excess verbiage.

In other words:

Shrink any task—by trimming its unnecessary parts.

It's like decluttering a room of furniture and accessories that are taking up valuable space.

How to Shrink Time

For most of us, time just seems to fly away.

In 1955, Cyril Northcote Parkinson began an article in *The Economist* with, "Work expands so as to fill the time available for its completion." This became known as Parkinson's law.

In other words, if you think it will take you an hour to write a memo, it will. But if all you have is thirty minutes, then that's all it will take!

So, amazingly:

> If you reduce the *amount of time* you give yourself to do something, you will often end up doing it—*on time!*

Deadlines push you to act efficiently.

How to Shrink Reading and Writing Too

Finally, I would like to share with you three techniques that I developed over the years, that helped cut down my reading and writing time—big time.

- *The Beginning-Captions-End Technique*

  This technique is an ideal approach for any text that *contains images.*

  It may be applied to most magazine and newspaper articles, whether digital or in print.

  The technique follows three quick steps:

  1. *First, read the beginning of the article*—the title and first paragraph.
  2. *Then read the captions*—under the images and the highlighted quotations in the text.
  3. *Then read the end of the article*—the last paragraph.

  Usually, you can get a pretty good idea of the main points in less than a minute. If it seems interesting, you can go back and read the article in detail later.

- *The Start-Skip Technique*

   This is ideal for reading any text that *doesn't contain images*.

   It's absolutely amazing that the majority of books are so full of superfluous content that can be skipped.

   The technique is simple:

   1. *As you start a paragraph*—decide whether you can guess what's coming in the rest of this paragraph or not.
   2. If you can—*just skip to the next one!*

   Using the *Start-Skip* technique will allow you to read any text in a quarter of the time it usually takes. You will get through three or four books in the same amount of time it would have taken you to read one.

- *The Voice Activation Technique*

   We talk so much faster than we can type. Voice-activation technology is a great way to save time when placing calls or dictating texts and e-mails.

RULE 6

in a Pearl Shell

Eliminate It, Delegate It, or Shrink It!
The Three Time-Management Secrets of Doing ...
What You Don't Have Time to Do

The First Secret of Time Management
The best way to do something *that doesn't need to be done ...*
is not to do it at all!
In other words: ***Eliminate it.***
- *Implement the Seven Smart Formulas*
  1 - Three Time-Windows; 2 - A Minute Is a Long Time;
  3 - Silenced Notifications; 4 - It's a Phone Ring, Not a
  Command; 5 - Block Unwanted Callers and E-mails;
  6 - Limit Social Media and Apps; 7 - Stop CC and Reply All
- *Eliminate Unnecessary E-mail Accounts*
- *Restrict TV Viewership and Non-essential Journal Subscriptions*

The Second Secret of Time Management
The best way to do something *you don't have to do personally ...*
is to let someone else do it for you!
In other words: ***Delegate it.***
- *Teach and Delegate, then Check and Re-Check*

RULE 6

in a Pearl Shell

The Third Secret of Time Management
If you can't eliminate it and can't delegate it . . .
then at least **shrink it!**
  • *Shrink Any Task*—by Trimming Its *Unnecessary* Parts
  • *Shrink the Time You Give Yourself to Do Something*—and You
    Will End Up Doing It *on Time!*
  • *Shrink Reading and Writing*—"Beginning-Captions-End,"
    "Start-Skip Paragraph," and "Voice Activation" Techniques

Then
You Will Have the Time *to Do . . .*
What You Really Want *to Do!*

DON'T DILUTE YOUR PRESENCE ... WITH TOO MUCH PRESENCE

The First Spoon of Honey Is a Delight, the Tenth Is a Turnoff!

A Jewel Called Aluminum

Would you believe that aluminum, one of the cheapest metals in the world today, was more precious than gold and silver in the nineteenth century?

In the mid-1800s, the price of aluminum was $550 per pound. It was so rare and so prized that it had been used in the making of a baby rattle commissioned for Crown Prince Louis-Napoléon.

Yet, fifty years later, the price of a pound of aluminum dropped to twenty-five cents. What started as a valuable commodity turned into something cheap and commonplace. And today, it's used to make the inexpensive tinfoil that we most often throw away.

How did a metal that was once more valuable than gold and silver became so ignoble? The answer is simple:

> **Aluminum was precious when it was ... scarce and hard to get!**

In the words of Olympic gold medalist Carli Lloyd, "Nothing in life is worthwhile unless it's kind of hard to get there."

In fact, prices for most products are determined by their availability and the level of desire for them in the marketplace.

It's all a matter of supply and demand.

Too much supply is what turned aluminum from a sought-after prized material into a cheap piece of metal. Similarly, too much supply is what makes having too much of a good thing, such as honey, undesirable.

That's exactly what will happen to you if you offer too much supply of your presence!

How to Keep a Crown Shining

No one knew the law of supply and demand better than Elizabeth II, the Queen of England.

Other than on annual celebrations such as Christmas Day, the monarch rarely addressed the nation. In fact, during her more-than-six-ty-nine-year reign, the Queen has appeared on a televised broadcast on just four occasions: The Gulf War, in 1991; the death of Princess Diana, in 1997; the death of the Queen Mother, in 2002; and the coronavirus pandemic, in 2020.

Plus, the Queen has never granted a press interview—in contrast to her children, who made numerous tell-all appearances to discuss their unhappy relationships. Why? Because the Queen always knew the value of *keeping her presence in scant supply.*

The Queen practiced the same principle when meeting dignitaries and guests. When she wanted a meeting with her prime minister to come to an end, she pressed a button and a butler immediately walked into the room to escort the prime minister out.

She has also been known to discreetly motion with her handbag when she wanted her staff to get her out of certain social situations at a moment's notice. She has been rumored to own more than two hundred Launer London bags, and has managed to turn them all into bye-bye bags! According to journalist Hugo Vickers, if the Queen popped her handbag on the table at dinner, it reportedly meant that she wanted the meal to end within five minutes. If it went on the floor, it meant that she was tired of the conversation and wanted to be whisked off quickly by her lady-in-waiting.

As Queen Elizabeth II restricted her presence, up went the demand for it. During a time when many monarchies have lost their luster or even vanished altogether, Queen Elizabeth, single-handedly, has ensured the robust survival of the British monarchy with all its appeal and mystique.

Not only did she save the crown, she even made it shinier!

David's Day

David is a forty-seven-year-old Chicago contractor and landlord who holds a degree in mechanical engineering. With two partners, Ron and Cheryl, he is the co-owner of a prestigious one-hundred-unit office building.

As David is meeting with his accountant for breakfast, his phone rings. It's a call from Cheryl. He hesitates a moment because he doesn't like to be interrupted. But then he reminds himself that Cheryl never calls unless it's important. So, he picks up the call.

And indeed, it's justified. She urgently needs some business advice. The call is short—three minutes. David then resumes his meeting.

Within the next hour, his cell phone rings twice. The first time it's a call from his other partner Ron, and the second time it's from an electrician, Bob, working on one of his construction sites.

He ignores both.

Why? Because he knows that Ron talks too much and that, once he gets going, he can easily chat for twenty minutes. It's a monologue. If David takes the call, he's stuck. Likewise, David knows that his electrician calls him multiple times a day for inconsequential queries that can wait. He could just as easily shoot David a quick text, but he never does. So, with both these callers, David figures that if they had something really important to discuss, they will call back.

On his way home, David picks up four bottles of wine. His wife, Silvia, is hosting a dinner party at eight for two neighborhood couples.

While driving, he gets a call from Sheila, a classmate from his university days. Two months earlier, she had called to say that she was in town for a conference and would love to meet for coffee. Delighted to hear from her after so many years, he invited her out for dinner, and they had a pleasant evening reminiscing about the good old days and catching up.

And now, just two months later, Sheila is calling again to give him the good news! She enthusiastically tells him that she will soon be passing through Chicago and would love to see him again.

Deep inside, David feels no excitement about the prospect of a second meeting with Sheila so soon after the first one. The anticipation he had felt at the first reunion just isn't there. He decides to avoid the encounter and finds an excuse to get out of it.

As he arrives home, the guests start showing up. The dinner goes well, followed by coffee and after-dinner drinks.

At 10 p.m., the Baxters, who arrived last, get up, thank David and his wife profusely, and leave. The Rossis, however, who arrived early, stay behind.

At 11 p.m., Silvia gets up, turns the music off and the lights up, and starts clearing the remaining glassware. The Rossis remain oblivious to these hints!

By 11:30 p.m., David has had it. He informs the Rossis, in a nice tone, that he is sorry, but he has to go to bed because of an early morning appointment. The Rossis are somewhat taken aback but downplay their shock and leave.

As soon as David is alone with his wife, he tells her, "The Rossis are entertaining and friendly, but we may have to reconsider inviting them again on a weekday. They overstayed their welcome."

It's always important to know when to leave the stage—and when enough is enough.

The Rossis didn't.

And if you behave as they did and make yourself too available, you will devalue yourself. People will take you for granted and won't appreciate your time or your presence.

On the other hand:

Anything that's in high demand—is more valuable.

So, view yourself as a valuable commodity. Make sure that others view you as such.

You can start by following the three lessons from David's story.

• *Calling*

Don't make the mistake David's associates did—*don't call too often or talk too long.*

A little can go a long way. Most calls can be handled in less than five minutes. Save longer conversations for a time when both sides can talk in person.

Relationships stay a lot fresher when you're not overloading them with too much conversation. In some instances, a quick text or an e-mail may be sufficient.

There are exceptions, of course. For example, if it's a parent or a close friend calling, you may want to take the call and take your time, even if it's inconvenient. Doing so is entirely justified, even honorable.

• *Meeting*

Don't make the mistake Sheila did—asking too early for a second get-together. She overreached, and that turned David off.

Be judicious about pacing your social get-togethers. Avoid the tendency to overload, even with persons close to you. Some people see their friends once or twice a month; others see them every few months.

It's wonderful to see people from all areas of your life, but not all the time, and not too frequently.

• *Staying*

Don't be like the Rossis, who arrived early and left late. They overstayed their welcome, and consequently became undesirable guests.

Don't overstay your welcome.

The bottom line is:

Remember when *enough is enough*.

Balance supply and demand when it comes to your presence. A little unavailability can go a long way. Build good fences around yourself and use them with friends, colleagues, and relatives.

And don't be "Too easy to get = just as easy to forget," as author Mandy Hale wrote.

Be hard to get!

RULE 7

in a Pearl Shell

Don't Dilute Your Presence . . . with Too Much Presence

The First Spoon of Honey Is a Delight, the Tenth Is a Turnoff!

- It's *Supply and Demand*
- *Don't Cheapen Your Presence* by Offering Too Much of It
- Know *When to Leave the Stage*, and *When Enough Is Enough*
- *Don't Call* Too Often, *Talk* for Too Long, or *Overstay* Your Welcome
- And Learn from the Aluminum Story: *Be Hard to Get!*

PUT YOUR PROBLEMS ON PAPER

*How to Solve Any Problem
in Less Than 5 Minutes*

Needed: A Brain Break

Your brain is a three-pound genius sitting inside your head. With its one hundred billion neurons, this wonder has the miraculous ability to figure out complex issues within just seconds.

But your brain does get tired. And every now and then, like you, it needs a break.

So, don't burden your brain with trivia. Only important issues and problems deserve your brainpower. Everything else doesn't.

Your brain doesn't need to be used as an appointment calendar or as a dumping ground for nonessential information. Reminders for doctor's appointments, haircuts, and birthdays, as well as information such as passport and driver's license numbers, should be relegated to your smartphone.

The "Whirlpool Whirling" Phenomenon

When you're faced with an important decision or problem, don't waste time by compulsively going over it in your head, reviewing its various implications multiple times.

This is brain harassment. And your brain will swiftly punish you with psychological distress.

When you worry about a problem repeatedly, you're churning through many of the thoughts you've already had. It's like watching the first half of a thriller multiple times without ever reaching the end. Or it's like being caught in an everlasting rinse-and-spin cycle that could blow your washing machine's fuse.

Ultimately, worrying turns your ideas into a whirlpool of disjointed turbulent thoughts that leave you worn out. The result? You're never able to resolve the problem.

So:

Stop the *Whirlpool Whirling!*

But then, what's the most efficient way to reach a speedy solution for a problem?

Here it is.

Behind Every Successful Person, There Is . . .

What do these successful people have in common: Bill Gates, Richard Branson, Tim Ferriss, and J. K. Rowling?

They all rely or relied on paper!

Many business leaders, illustrious artists, and high achievers share the habit of using pen and paper to document, analyze, and process ideas.

Mark Zuckerberg was once giving a lecture to aspiring entrepreneurs in Silicon Valley. According to writer Ben Casnocha, the auditorium was packed. In the front row sat two legendary investors, John Doerr and Ron Conway. They both stood out, not only because of their grayish hair, but also because they were the only two audience members *taking notes on paper.* The novices didn't see the point!

Bill Gates, Microsoft cofounder, is a regular user of pen and paper despite his computer skills. According to technology executive Rob Howard, who attended a meeting with him, he "didn't bring a computer in with him, but instead [was] taking notes on a yellow pad of paper."

Richard Branson, the billionaire business magnate, is known for having said, "I always have a notebook on hand. I can't tell you where I'd be if I hadn't had a pen on hand to write down my ideas."

And J. K. Rowling is known to have written the first drafts of all her unforgettable Harry Potter books in longhand.

You wonder: Why do all these successful individuals, as well as many others, choose paper over keyboards?

Here's the answer.

Back from the Dead

Within the last few years, handwritten notes have become increasingly rare.

When you check your mailbox nowadays, how often do you get a handwritten letter? Spiral notebooks and pens, once common, are vanishing as smartphones, laptops, and touch-screen tablets become the norm.

Is longhand dead and buried? Should pens and notebooks be housed in a museum? Many young people are downright embarrassed to be seen with them. Should you be too?

Not so fast. It seems that old-fashioned pen and paper may still have advantages after all.

In an article titled "The Pen Is Mightier Than the Keyboard: Advantages of Longhand Over Laptop Note Taking," published in the journal *Psychological Science*, professors Pam A. Mueller of Princeton University and Daniel M. Oppenheimer of UCLA sought to test the effectiveness of taking notes by hand as opposed to typing them into a computer.

Surprisingly, the results of their study showed that:

Students taking notes longhand performed much better than those typing on laptops.

The authors theorized that because students using laptops can type faster than they write, they were likely to try to transcribe every word they heard. As a result, they largely engaged in mindless transcription and didn't have time to absorb the material that was being taught. This shallow cognitive practice ended up being detrimental to their learning.

On the other hand, the *students taking longhand notes were forced to process what they heard and reframe it in their own words.* While processing the material, these students had to choose which elements were important to write down, thereby embedding these aspects more firmly into their memory banks.

The German philosopher Hermann Ebbinghaus, who described what's now known as the "Ebbinghaus curve," found that we forget around 40 percent of what we read or hear by the following day. So, in order to improve memory and recall, active rather than passive learning is necessary.

Active learning requires that students do something that develops their skills through problem solving and reflection, which promote critical thinking; as opposed to passive learning, in which information is merely related to them. This is why the longhand writers did significantly better than their computer-using counterparts.

In sum:

Note taking by hand—promotes active learning.

Active learning is far superior to passive learning because it's an engaging strategy that requires mental effort, concentration and the reframing of information. And the greater the processing, the stronger the recall.

David Sax, author of *The Revenge of Analog*, advocates the longhand system because, in addition to having a recall advantage, it "requires no power source, no boot-up time, no program-specific formatting, and no syncing to external drives and the cloud."

Still, it might be a hard sell to get people to go back to pen and paper. Fortunately, multiple new devices allow users to write with a stylus, which is essentially just another type of pen!

Focus Is Key

Now, back to my earlier question: What's the most efficient way to dissect a problem and reach a speedy solution to it?

You may have guessed by now. It can be summarized in just one word: paper!

It's simple: You need to write down your problem and evaluate it on paper.

This often works like magic. *It's amazing how much easier it is to focus on solving a problem when it is written on a piece of paper, in front of you, instead of churning it again and again in your head.* This helps you better understand the problem by visualizing its roots in a more rational way, allowing you to see what you can do to deal with it through multiple options. And it's also an instant stress releaser.

When it comes to solving problems:

Focus is crucial, and paper is key to focus.

The "5-Minute" Formula

"A problem clearly stated is a problem half solved," asserted writer Dorothea Brande.

That's essentially what this "5-Minute" Formula does in four simple steps:
1. write the *problem* down on a piece of paper;
2. write down *all possible solutions* (every option you can think of, even if you dislike some of them);
3. *compare* the solutions; and then
4. *choose* the best one.

Here is an example of the "5-Minute" Formula in action:

First, let's say you *state your problem* as follows: I can't find time to organize my personal financial records.

Second, *write down all possible solutions*, even the least likely options, as they come to your mind, in no particular order:
1. Delegate this to my accountant.
2. Delegate this to my son, who is good at organizing.
3. Ask my spouse for her help in taking care of it.
4. Use tax-preparation software.
5. Query friends, family, and colleagues about how they handle their records.

Third, *go over the options, circling the reasonable ones and crossing out the impractical ones.* The goal is to narrow them down to a few that best fit your situation.

Let's say that in this case, you decide to *circle options 2 and 3.*

Finally, *go over the circled options and choose the best one.* Say you choose option 3 because you trust your spouse most with handling your finances.

Done. Problem solved!

Remember, don't take much longer than five minutes to go through this process. Otherwise, you will overthink, overwrite, and lose momentum.

What's the optimal time of the day to employ the "5-Minute" Formula? My suggestion is bedtime because all daily tasks have been done by then, and you can concentrate without distraction.

So, before going to bed, take five minutes and go through the preceding four steps using a notebook you can keep by the bed. Once you finish this short practical exercise, you can fall asleep happily.

I know some people may be tempted to write out their thoughts on their smartphones, tablets, or computers. But remember that handwriting is far superior to typing in terms of processing ideas.

The other problem with a keyboard is that as long as you have the device in your hands, you may want to check your e-mails and social media feeds, which can prevent you from falling asleep. And keeping electronics near your bed is bad for your health in a number of ways.

So, no keyboards please.

Trip on Track ✓, but Destination Unknown

Just imagine that someone gets into his car and drives, as fast as possible, anxious to reach his destination.

There is only one problem: he doesn't know his destination!

In his mind, he has many possibilities: the shopping center, the office, the movie theater, the gym, or the beach, but he isn't sure which one to choose. Yet, he keeps pressing on the gas pedal and driving forward at full speed.

That driver was me!

When I first started my medical practice, I was willing to do whatever it took to make it successful. But as I prepared for the opening, I felt overwhelmed. I was exerting substantial effort, and my adrenaline was surging. I felt unfocused, with no one particular goal in mind. In short, I felt lost.

Faced with this hurdle, I turned to the "5-Minute" Formula.

As I went to bed one night, I pulled out my notebook and opened it on a new page. (I still have that page. I've saved all my notebooks over the years.) Then, I wrote out my problem and all the possible solutions:

Problem: What's my top goal for my practice?

Possibilities:

1. Build a large practice with a big clientele.
2. Earn a high income.

3. Establish a good reputation in the community and among my peers.

4. Perform high-quality surgery.

5. Arrange to have enough time for my family and leisure activities.

They all seemed very important to me. But I still had to go through a process of elimination—*circling* the reasonable options and *crossing out* the unreasonable ones. Eventually, I narrowed my options down to options 4 and 5.

As I reflected on option 5, I felt that the amount of time I spent with my wife, Stephanie, and our two little kids, Amanda and Michael, was already fairly substantial.

So, I settled on option 4—perform high-quality surgery—as my main goal.

However, this top goal was still too vague. So, I went back to the notebook and repeated the process.

Problem: How can I perform high-quality surgery?

Possibilities:

1. Take plenty of time during each procedure.

2. Attend multiple courses and conferences.

3. Achieve natural results.

4. Hire top assistants in the operating room.

5. Use minimally invasive surgical techniques.

6. Use minimally invasive anesthesia techniques.

Again, all options seemed important. But as in all areas of life, the hard part was to zoom in on the most important.

After a process of elimination, I reduced the six options to three—namely, 3, 5, and 6. These became the mini goals of my one main goal—*high-quality surgery.*

And ever since that day, I have been devoting a disproportionate amount of time and attention to those three mini goals:

• *Achieve natural results*

This became an obsession of mine, and it's the goal I mention most often in my presentations at medical conferences and during interviews.

- *Use minimally invasive surgical techniques*

  I published an article about a new concept in cosmetic surgery called "Optimum Mobility," a scientific approach that reduces the need for aggressive procedures. I also introduced multiple techniques that use small mini-incisions for multiple procedures such as nasal surgery (rhinoplasty), forehead lifts, breast augmentations, and facelifts.

- *Use minimally invasive anesthesia techniques*

  I've managed to avoid general anesthesia in all my face and body cosmetic surgeries by using a sophisticated combination of sedatives administered under advanced monitoring systems.

  Once I pinpointed my main goal and its mini goals, my destination was known. And ever since, I have never stopped driving full speed toward it!

A Priority List—Prior to All

If you want to hire an accountant, you certainly wouldn't attempt to interview every accountant in town.

You would first need to decide what you're looking for in such a person: A specific fee range? A particular kind of service? A certain number of years of experience? Good references?

Only after completing your list of priorities and knowing what you're looking for can you then begin searching for the right person.

The same principle applies to anything you're pursuing in life.

So, before making a decision about a purchase, a vacation, a life direction or even a romantic relationship, write down what you're looking for, then prioritize these elements.

For example, before you search for a new house, write down your priorities, in order of priority:

- maximum price: $1,000,000
- near downtown
- minimum three bedrooms

- on the lake
- facing south
- maximum age: fifteen years
- two-car garage

Only after you have this list in hand can you start shopping for a house.

And the same formula applies to looking for a new dress, a new employer, or whatever it is you're wanting to do or acquire.

The Little Ones

Finally, I have a little trick I would like to share with you.

I keep pads of paper and pens everywhere at home—in the bedroom, bathroom, study, kitchen and living room—as well as in my car and on my office desk.

Why? Suppose as I'm getting dressed in the morning, I remember that I need to buy a gift for a friend. Rather than looking for my phone so I can enter this as a reminder, I simply pick up a small piece of paper nearby and write one word—*gift*—on it, and put it in my pocket.

Later that day, when I come back home and empty my pockets for the day, I can take the time to add the reminder to a to-do list on my phone, or just put that paper note under a paperweight on top of, say, a triple dresser as a constant physical reminder.

The same system applies to notes I make at the office. If I'm asked by a colleague to find information or finish part of a project, I just write down one or two words on a handy small piece of paper and keep it in a paper clip on my desk, which I check first thing in the morning and last thing before leaving.

As you become better at using both screens and paper for tasks and reminders, you will opt instinctively for the approach most practical and comfortable for you.

RULE 8

in a Pearl Shell

Put Your Problems on Paper
How to Solve Any Problem in Less Than 5 Minutes

- Don't Burden Your Brain with Trivia
- *Stop the "Whirlpool Whirling"*
- When Facing a Problem, *Use the "5-Minute" Formula—on Paper*
- Keep Your Trip on Track ✓, with Destination Known
- *Make Your Priority List*
- Keep *Notepads* Handy

WHAT'S THE WORST-CASE SCENARIO?

And What's the Most Probable One?

A Little Storm

We tend to be easily disturbed by all kinds of little problems that cause us a great deal of grief and distress.

Small events become exaggerated in our minds, blown out of proportion, causing us to worry and obsess over details, while missing the big picture.

However, with time, we end up discovering that most of these temporary predicaments are trivial—nothing more than fleeting annoyances, with little or no long-term impact on our lives.

It's *useless*—to worry about *useless* things!

For example, you spill some red wine on your cream-colored carpet; you discover a nasty scratch on your new car; you lose your favorite pen; you receive a parking ticket; you miss your flight.

Such inconveniences seem drastic in the moment and upset you. But sooner or later, you will realize just how puny they are, in the grand scheme of things. A few months later, these small-scale calamities become meaningless as their significance fades. They are gone and forgotten, as if they never happened. It's only in hindsight that you will recognize how transient your present mishaps really are.

So, here is a dictum of life:

An insignificant problem—
is one you won't remember *6 months* from now.

It initially feels like a turbulent storm, with you swirling in its midst. But as time goes by, you will realize that the whole thing was nothing more than *a little tempest in a little teapot.*

Therefore, when you're faced with any momentary inconvenience or a mini crisis, ask yourself: *Will I remember it in six months?*

If the answer is no, get over it on the spot. Accept what happened, try to find a sensible solution to it (by using your paper and pen!), then let it go. You simply don't have time to waste on inconsequential matters.

And don't let those frivolous events distract you from all the blessings you have.

Appreciate the good things in life and enjoy them now—today. You never know what tomorrow can bring. You may one day realize how lucky you were, even when you were bent out of shape over unimportant things.

You will then regret every single minute you spent worrying about those insignificant little storms.

A Big Storm

Have you ever heard the quotation, "My life has been filled with terrible misfortunes, most of which never happened"? The Renaissance philosopher Michel de Montaigne is supposed to have said this five hundred years ago. And it still rings true today.

And haven't you noticed that many of the things you worry about most end up being a waste of your time and energy? Researchers at the University of Cincinnati found that 85 percent of the imagined calamities we envision will never happen at all.

This reminds me of one of my patients, Tania, who once left me a message over a weekend saying that she had an emergency and needed to see me ASAP. She had had a blepharoplasty (eyelid surgery) a few months earlier.

When she arrived at the clinic early Monday morning, she looked terrified. She pointed out a mole on her cheek. She was sure she didn't have this lesion before her operation and was convinced it was skin cancer.

It wasn't! The lesion was benign. I even showed Tania the same mole in her preoperative photos from months earlier. Only then did she realize that she feared and fretted all weekend long for nothing.

So, it's true that many of the things we worry about most end up being a waste of our time and energy

However, at other times, what we are dealing with could be truly serious.

Out of the blue, we may get hit with a tumultuous event—being diagnosed with a serious illness, losing a job, going through a divorce, suffering an investment loss, facing a family crisis, experiencing emotional abandonment, or enduring any other major reversal of fortune. These severe life trials cause us fear, anxiety, and sadness. They can easily overwhelm us and take a profound toll on our stress levels and our sense of happiness.

For example, being sued is a scary experience for anyone. Your first response is probably panic, anger, and fear. You keep thinking of all the terrible things that could happen: you may have to spend a lot of money on lawyers; your reputation could be tarnished; you might lose all your savings and go bankrupt; you might even wind up in prison.

These radical scenarios and projections into the future run rampant in your head like a horror movie as your stress level skyrockets. These can drive you crazy. They may even make you physically ill.

It has been proven that anxiety is linked to heart disease, cancer, shrinking brain mass, and premature aging, not to mention marital problems, family dysfunction, and depression.

We've got to keep a handle on our worries. Is there a way to control these mental demons so that we can increase our chances of living longer and happier lives?

Yes, there is.

One Big Storm, but Two Weather Forecasts

When faced in life with a seemingly big storm, treat it as you would any other problem:

Put It on Paper (Rule 8).

Use a notebook, ideally at bedtime, and spend no more than five minutes jotting down the answer to each of the following "two weather forecasts" questions:

> **What's the worst-case scenario?**
> **And what's the most probable scenario?**

In the majority of cases, you will be surprised to discover that:

> **The worst-case scenario,**
> **though upsetting, isn't the end of the world.**
> **In addition, *it's improbable.***

Your life won't end. Your children won't abandon you.

Similarly, you might discover that:

> **The most probable scenario**
> **isn't that bad at all.**
> **In addition, *it's the one most likely to happen.***

Once you have both scenarios on paper, in black and white, you will feel relieved.

So:

> **Expect the *probable* ...**
> **while realizing that you could still survive the *improbable.***

When Mango Went from Yucky to Yummy

Early in my career, I was invited to attend the annual conference of the International Society of Aesthetic Surgery in Tokyo.

I was asked to give two talks, one on revision rhinoplasty (operating on a nose that had an unsuccessful surgery in the past), and another one on expression plasty (a science I developed that analyzes unwanted facial expressions).

My wife, Stephanie, was joining me on the trip and suggested that we stop in Thailand and Singapore on the way over to Japan. I happily agreed.

Our three-day stay in Bangkok was spent at an exotic hotel called the Oriental. The food there was delicious, especially the mango juice and the abundant mango desserts. Mango has always been my favorite fruit.

On our second day, before going down for breakfast, I decided to phone my Montreal office to check on the practice. My then office manager, Louise, told me that Patricia, a patient of mine who had had a facelift two weeks earlier, was complaining of sudden swelling and redness on one side of her face. I told Louise to have the covering surgeon examine her and prescribe antibiotics as required. I also said that I would call back in two days to make sure things were okay.

As I hung up the phone and went down for breakfast, I started to worry. In fact, I lost my appetite, even for the mango juice. I told Stephanie that I was thinking seriously of returning to Montreal because I felt tense about being so far away from home should my patient need me.

As we went out that morning to visit the magnificent Grand Palace, I simply couldn't enjoy it. My mind was racing with worries about what could or would go wrong with my patient. By dinnertime that night, I was totally out of sorts.

Finally, I remembered the "two weather forecasts" questions (sometimes, I forget my own rules—but not for long!). So, at bedtime, I took out my notebook and answered the two questions:

Q: What's the worst thing that could happen to my patient?

A: Based on Patricia's symptoms, the worst possibility would be an abscess that could be drained through the original incision. The great majority of such rare cases heal extremely well, especially since my facelift technique is a very conservative one.

Q: What's the most probable outcome of Patricia's predicament?

A: In all likelihood, Patricia will get better within a few days, especially since she has no fever or pain.

As I looked at my two options on paper, I felt as if a fresh breeze had washed over me. By answering these two questions in writing, I was able to use my rational mind rather than being driven by primal emotions.

I was so relieved that I ordered both a mango juice and a mango dessert from room service. Stephanie was so thrilled that she joined in the celebration.

It was mango galore!

And by the way, Patricia recovered fully!

The Beyond Tragic

There are, however, some situations in which the "two weather forecasts" formula won't apply—when the problem is beyond serious, beyond sad.

Some examples are: if someone we love passes away; if we are diagnosed with a very serious illness; or if we experience a profound calamity that can't be rectified, whether at work, in a relationship, or with our finances.

In all such situations, when the outcome is very grim, then, unfortunately this formula isn't going to help.

Beyond sad is beyond any universal rules.

But maybe not beyond God, if you're a believer.

"For nothing will be impossible with God" (Luke 1:37).

RULE 9

in a Pearl Shell

What's the Worst-Case Scenario?
And What's the Most Probable One?

Just Follow the Weather!

For a Little Storm, Ask Yourself:
- *Will I Remember It 6 Months Down the Road?*
  It's *Useless* to Worry About *Useless* Things

For a Big Storm, Ask Yourself:
- *What's the Worst-Case Scenario?*
  Often, It *Isn't the End of the World,* and It's *Improbable*
- *What's the Most Probable Scenario?*
  Often, It *Isn't that Bad,* and It's *Most Likely* to Happen

YOUR #1 GOAL IN LIFE IS HAPPINESS

How to Implement the Four Indispensable Secrets of Living Happily

The "Table with Four Legs" Phenomenon

Ask anyone what he or she wants most in life, and the answer you will probably get is—happiness.

But happiness is defined differently by everyone who seeks it. When I make appearances at conferences to present my universal rules, I am always surprised and amused by the audience responses when I ask, "What are the secrets of happiness?"

Some of the most typical responses define success as a prerequisite for happiness, whether that means an accumulation of wealth, status or professional recognition. Others mention the importance of good physical health, self-actualization, or religious faith. Still others suggest a fulfilling work, a passionate romantic relationship, a compatible marriage, or the joy of having children.

But what is happiness, exactly?

In my view, happiness is a predominant feeling that life is good. You're happy when you experience a consistent sense of well-being, a glow, a daily enjoyment of life, and the anticipation of having something to look forward to.

But how to achieve this?

For many years, I was intrigued with the question: What makes happy people happy?

The answer seemed, at first, elusive. However, over the years, I have settled on what I believe to be the absolute and indispensable *four pillars of happiness.* Without any one of these four pillars, happiness becomes unstable and wobbly, and ultimately topples over, like a table missing one of its four legs.

So, here they are, The Four Secrets of Happiness.

THE FIRST SECRET OF HAPPINESS
Working and Keeping Busy
Happiness Isn't Owning Things ... but Doing Things!

Getting Up in the Morning: Then What?

Most of us are obsessed with owning things.

These may include a new home, a luxurious car, the latest electronic devices, jewelry, designer clothes, sought-after artwork, cash or securities. It's a sparkly world full of riches and precious items that consume our popular culture, and end up consuming us.

However, the problem with this is that—*once we have acquired these things, the enjoyment they bring fades quickly.* For example, no matter how excited you are about your new car on the day you bought it, you will become blasé about it within a few weeks or months. The novelty of it simply wears off.

This is because:

> No object—once obtained—can keep you perpetually entertained.

Therefore:

> What's important isn't what you *own*—it's what you *do*.

It's your activities that keep you alive and interested in life. When you're physically and mentally active, it's a form of self-entertainment that's essential to boosting your feel-good state and keeping you energetic and engaged.

> Working and keeping busy—give you purpose.

They allow you to have *somewhere* to go in the morning, *someone* to meet, and *something* to look forward to, in addition to making you feel useful.

It's not about hedonism, pleasure seeking, or a collection of shiny objects. In fact, UCLA researchers, in collaboration with University of

North Carolina scientists, confirmed that happiness is derived from having a sense of purpose in life.

For some of us, just waking up every morning at a specific time, getting dressed and leaving the house gives us an objective for the day. For others, working at home, looking after children, going shopping, cooking, cleaning the house, or volunteering within the community are all valuable tasks that keep us fulfilled and satisfied.

> **When we aren't busy—we feel bored, deflated, and useless.**

That's why some retirees, even affluent ones, lose their will to live— because they don't feel useful, wanted, or needed. They don't have anything to get up for in the morning, nothing to occupy their days. If they don't have that, what good will a luxury car or a seaside mansion do them? How happy can they be just getting up, eating something, watching TV, and spending the rest of the day drifting from one small task to another, with no schedule and no responsibilities? Nothing could be more antithetical to happiness.

Working and the Now
Working is a negativity buster.

> **When you're busy—you have no time for skepticism!**

You don't have the luxury of dwelling on feelings of worry, sadness, loneliness, despair, anger, resentment, or jealousy—the demons of unhappiness. You spend much less mental energy obsessing about the future and remembering past unpleasant events.

> **When you're busy—you're engaged in the *now*.**

And you're more creative and mentally alert.

When a Vacation Is So Boring

You surely have noticed that:

> **The harder you work during the week—
> the more you enjoy the weekend.**

That's because there is a therapeutic contrast between the challenge of work and the release you experience when you let loose and relax. The frenetic energy of workdays contrasts with the freedom and laziness of vacations. "It is the joy of work well done that enables us to enjoy rest," wrote author Elisabeth Elliot.

> **You appreciate *doing nothing*—
> only when it's preceded by *doing something!***

Too much time off can make your weekends meaningless and your vacations boring. In other words, happiness doesn't exist without the yin and yang of hard work followed by relaxation.

Therefore, staying busy is a critical stepping-stone on the magical pathway to happiness.

THE SECOND SECRET OF HAPPINESS
Having Exciting Expectations
*Happiness Is the Yellow Brick Road to the Exciting
Goal . . . that Ends Once You Reach That Goal!*

A Wiz of a Wiz, If Ever a Wiz There Was

In the classic Hollywood film *The Wizard of Oz*, Dorothy sets out on the journey of a lifetime, following the enchanted Yellow Brick Road on her quest to meet the Wizard of Oz in the Emerald City.

It's an adventure filled with multiple twists and turns: the threat of the Wicked Witch of the West; the delight of the Munchkins; Dorothy's heartfelt relationships with the Tin Man, the Scarecrow, and the Cowardly Lion; and her ultimate redemption by the Good Witch of the North. Through it all, Dorothy never loses her desire to reach her goal.

We all need an Emerald City in our lives—a Wizard to seek.

We all need thrilling expectations—pleasurable goals that galvanize us and move us forward in life.

> **Thrilling expectations**
> **give us ... something to look forward to in the future.**

The mere anticipation of them fosters happiness. We all feel good and excited when we're preparing for a joyous event, whether it's a cruise, a summer vacation, starting a new job, moving into a new house, a wedding, or a baby. All these things spell enjoyment and fulfillment on multiple levels.

So, if you're feeling annoyed, frustrated, or bored, having inspirational goals will provide you with motivation and persistence. They will give meaning to the future, because you know there is a reward waiting for you just up ahead. They mobilize you to perform and persevere.

You look forward to today and tomorrow, and you anticipate exhilarating prospects beyond tomorrow.

Less Is More, Sometimes
Your goals don't have to be big.

It's important to choose reasonably motivating but realistic goals, rather than grandiose ones that are doomed from the start.

No matter how small or trifling, exciting goals promise a payoff in good feelings. It can be something as modest as the anticipation of a holiday weekend, a dinner date, a meet-up with friends, a birthday party, a movie, or a coffee break.

When you have something to look forward to, even if it's the relaxation of a little nap, it will give you the strength to power through your daily problems, and will keep you eager to surmount your present challenges, while on your way to achieving those attractive dreams. These simple expectations work as energizing pills in your life and carry you through thick and thin.

Done, Now What?

Your goals need to be continually refreshed.

> A goal—once achieved—isn't exciting anymore!

You now need to find another appealing expectation to embark upon. In other words:

> Happiness is the excitement you feel
> while moving toward a stimulating *goal*...
> but it ends once you reach that *goal!*

Because once the anticipated target is ultimately achieved, it has passed. You lose the ten pounds—and then what? You get the promotion at work—and then what?

Therefore, you have to keep moving past your realized expectation and head toward another exciting one. It's like Dorothy's enchanted trip to Oz, which led her to the end of one adventure and the beginning of another.

You can't rest on your laurels. *Your life should be a succession of exciting goals.*

THE THIRD SECRET OF HAPPINESS
Staying Healthy
*The Crucial Steps for Prevention and Early Detection
of Cancer, Heart Disease, Diabetes, and Alzheimer's Disease*

It's Vice Versa

One key component of happiness is good physical and mental health.

If you're sick, it's difficult to feel happy. Imagine how it would feel to suffer from chronic pain or battle a major illness. Faced with such challenges, it's hard to enjoy life.

Good health feeds happiness, and vice versa—happiness feeds good health. In other words, happiness and health are intertwined. One enhances the other. Numerous scientific studies reveal that happiness has major health benefits. It combats stress, boosts the immune system, and increases life expectancy.

Therefore, our duty is to do everything we possibly can to remain healthy, both physically and psychologically.

Physical Health

In the following section, I will be discussing a general concept of prevention and treatment.

This approach, however, may not apply to you. What's best for one person may not be best for another. And what's best today may be unsuitable tomorrow. Everything changes with time, almost on a daily basis, as new studies and new discoveries emerge.

So, check with your physician first and with your common sense second.

Before, Not After: The Art of Prevention

It's surprising how many of us assign a low priority to physical health.

The Chinese philosopher and taijiquan master Chungliang Huang was right when he said that many people treat their bodies as if they were rented cars—something they use to get around in, but nothing they care about understanding!

However, to give our happiness an insurance policy, it's imperative that we take the well-being of our bodies seriously.

An investment in *wellness*—is a prevention of *illness,*
and a prevention of *illness*—is an investment in *happiness*!

This means it's important to take advantage of every reliable medical diagnostic and therapeutic tool available. Doing so will help protect the body and mind, which will, in turn, keep us healthy and more likely to be happy.

The progress of twenty-first-century medical technology is breathtaking, allowing the kind of diagnostic analysis that was unthinkable just a decade ago, as well as new cures for many illnesses.

All these amazing medical cures are great, but:

> The best cure of all—
> is prevention and early detection.

Early Cancer Detection

Early cancer detection can be lifesaving—literally.

Believe it or not, our chances of getting cancer at some point in our lifetimes is very high—almost 50 percent.

Cancer is so deadly because it can grow in the body insidiously, silently and unnoticed for years. Accordingly, it's often not discovered until we start having symptoms. By then, it may be too late. Yet, early cancer detection testing is often underestimated and underperformed.

There are several modern techniques that increase your chances of detecting cancer early:

- *New Blood Tests*
  Some of these are already available in North America and Europe, and new ones are constantly introduced. Though expensive, they are well worth it.

- *Radiological Total-body Screening*
  MRIs and ultrasounds, both of which involve no radiation, are ideal options for early detection of a cancer mass.

- *Laparoscopies*
  These tests use scopes to look directly inside accessible cavities, such as the stomach (gastroscopy) and the colon (colonoscopy), to check for any abnormalities or masses.

All these tests may be repeated every few years, depending on a person's age.

Checkups and Tests

Regular annual medical checkups and routine laboratory tests are musts for early detection and maintenance of multiple diseases such as diabetes, high blood pressure, high cholesterol, anemia, leukemia, and many others.

Good Nutrition

"Thou should eat to live, not live to eat," wrote Socrates.

Yet many of us gorge ourselves on rich foods and alcohol, or allow our impulses to go wild with the overconsumption of sugary or fried foods.

Although there are still important differences of opinion among scientists, the basic characteristics of healthful foods and drinks that most, but not all, authorities agree upon may be simplified briefly in seven points:

• *Organic Food*

Organic food is often fresher than conventionally-grown or -raised food, contains fewer pesticides, and doesn't have preservatives.

As well, locally grown organic produce has been proven to be more nutritious as they are fresher, and therefore nutrient-dense, compared to foods that have traveled far and long, which cause them to lose some of their nutritious value.

• *Little or No Sugar*

Sugar is detrimental to cellular health and is loaded with calories.

• *Little or No Processed Food*

Processed foods often contain large quantities of sugar, fat, salt, and calories.

• *Moderate or No Alcohol*

Red wine is generally preferred.

- *Seafood*
Seafood is generally preferred over chicken and red meat—in that order.
- *Blue Zones Foods*
Dan Buettner, in his books about blue zones—areas of the world where people live the longest—identifies the foods and beverages most often consumed in these regions, including beans, fresh vegetables, nuts, olive oil, spices (turmeric, pepper), green and herbal teas, certain breads (rye, barley, sourdough), red wine, fish, almond and coconut milks, brown rice, feta cheese, fresh fruit, and lots of water.

All the preceding suggestions differ among various scientific schools and change over time.

Multivitamins and Supplements
Although not everyone agrees on the benefits of supplements, an increasing number of medical trials are proving their worth.

Popular supplements include vitamin D3, omega-3 fatty acids, curcumin, CoQ10, probiotics, resveratrol, folate, magnesium, alpha-lipoic acid, astaxanthin, vitamin E, vitamin B12, Boswellia, vitamin K, iodine, and others.

However, the rating and perceived safety of each supplement may change as newer studies are conducted.

Exercise
Physical exercise is essential to good health.

Exercise reduces the risk of heart attacks, protects against some types of cancers, regulates insulin levels, decreases the risk of type 2 diabetes, boosts metabolism and fat loss, lowers cholesterol levels and blood pressure, improves muscle strength and endurance, stabilizes joints, strengthens bones, improves posture, lowers inflammation, deepens sleep, and enhances mood and energy levels.

There are three basic types of physical exercise:

- *Sports*

Some people consider recreational sports, such as tennis, golf, skiing, jogging, cycling, baseball, volleyball, basketball, football, softball, soccer, or hockey, to be sufficient exercise for maintaining vibrant health.

This is true, but only if one already has strong muscles.

In other words, although sports are excellent for the cardiovascular system (heart and circulation), they require strong muscles to begin with. Otherwise, sports can exert detrimental stress on vulnerable joints, such as knees, ankles, elbows, hips, and shoulders. That's because all joints depend on robust muscles for their protection when subjected to strenuous use.

Many frail elderly people are in wheelchairs, not just due to their weak heart, but often because of their *weak muscles*, which led to *weak joints*, which led to *restricted mobility.*

Therefore, sports should be either preceded or accompanied by muscle-building exercises. No matter how old you are, obtain good advice from a professional trainer to build your muscles through weight training before engaging in recreational sports.

- *Weight Training*

Strong muscles are a must for strong joints, and both are invaluable for a good quality of life.

Weight training builds strong muscles. You must create resistance to muscular contraction in order to build muscle volume and endurance. This is accomplished by lifting free weights or using resistance-training machines.

For muscles to gain volume and strength, this type of training needs to be done regularly—weekly at a minimum.

- *Aerobics*

Aerobic exercise, even a light version of it, increases the efficiency of the respiratory and cardiovascular systems.

You don't have to complete a marathon or a triathlon to benefit from aerobics. Walking at a brisk, energetic pace is easy to do and practical. Swimming, biking, or anything that quickens your breathing and heart rate is beneficial.

Especially helpful is another habit—taking the stairs instead of the elevator. So, whenever you see an elevator or an escalator, *opt for the stairs instead*, which can usually be found nearby.

Finally, my *first Universal Rule—Do It Now, Perfect It Later—* applies to all these types of exercises. Even a few minutes a day is better than nothing.

Mental Activity

Being physically healthy is the foundation of a healthy brain.

But that's not enough. Keeping your brain active is paramount in preventing cerebral decline. It's key to staying alert and feeling happy.

Working and keeping busy (the absolute best) and reading are two great tools for brain stimulation and preservation. Other ways to exercise the brain include puzzles and strategic games such as chess, backgammon, and cards. You could also take a dance class, find a volunteering opportunity, study a foreign language, or learn a new skill such as playing a musical instrument, painting, sculpting, carpentry, or gardening.

You just have to keep doing something—anything—to stay mentally stimulated.

Avoiding Physical Risks

It may seem unbelievable, but millions of us jeopardize our lives on a daily basis—almost deliberately.

In the United States alone, around thirty-four million adults smoke cigarettes, which has been proven to cause cancer.

Legions of others text while driving, which surprisingly leads to about 1.6 million crashes per year, causes half a million injuries, and claims six thousand lives.

Then there is the use and abuse of legal and illegal drugs, as well as excessive alcohol intake.

And what about exposure to the sun? More than four million cases of basal cell carcinoma, a type of skin cancer, are diagnosed in the

United States each year, many of them linked to sun exposure. This, as well, leads to premature skin aging and cataracts in the eye.

To avoid or diminish these negative side effects, we can stay in the shade while outdoors, and wear a hat, sunglasses, and sunscreen.

There are also other obvious risks to keep at bay, such as damaging loud noises (in nightclubs and concert venues), which can injure the inner ears, leading to hearing loss, ringing of the ears (tinnitus), and sensitivity to sound.

Finally, you can take other simple precautions to safeguard your health, such as avoiding pollution, staying away from dark streets, protecting your home with an alarm system, holding railings while going up and down stairs, and never driving when you're sleepy or too tired.

These are just a few examples of behaviors that you need to implement. Nothing is worth the risk of injury, paralysis, disfigurement, or disability.

Controlling Body Weight

Avoiding obesity at all costs is crucial.

Obesity may lead to type 2 diabetes, high blood pressure, sleep apnea, respiratory disorders, heart disease, cancer, stroke, acid reflux, and bone and joint damage. And that's just the short list.

Try adopting whatever diet protocol works for you, be it intermittent fasting (my favorite), a low-carbohydrate regimen, or any other nutrition plan that suits you.

Most important, opt for one that can be sustained.

Managing Snoring

Most people view snoring as an annoying but trivial condition. It isn't.

Snoring is an underestimated dysfunction that occurs when the flow of air through the nose and mouth becomes restricted at the back of the throat. It may be caused by anatomical obstruction, age, or obesity. It can lead to adverse health effects, including daytime fatigue and heart disease, because less air entering the lungs means less oxygen in the blood, and therefore less oxygen in the organs, including the heart and, especially, the brain.

Many people who snore loudly have obstructive sleep apnea, the recurrent interruption of breathing for a few seconds or longer during sleep. The treatment involves a small CPAP (continuous positive airway pressure) device that pushes air through the nose with enough power to reach the lungs in adequate volume.

When I started snoring a couple of years before I began writing this book, I went to a specialist for a sleep test. Thankfully, it indicated that I had very mild obstructive sleep apnea that didn't necessarily require treatment. However, after close analysis, it was discovered that the level of oxygen in my blood (O2 saturation) was lowering repeatedly a little during the night, just below the ideal level. I thought that if my brain is deprived of even a little oxygen every single night, it could be affected over the long term. After starting on a CPAP device, I felt more energetic and well rested each morning. And I am still using it to this day.

If you snore, consider having a sleep test and being evaluated for possible treatment.

Psychological Health

To be happy, we have to maintain our emotional health and psychological well-being.

But how should we define emotional health?

In my opinion, it's about how we think, how we feel, how we behave, how life affects us, and how we cope with adversity.

And the main tool for achieving good psychological health is avoiding and preventing stress—which, as studies have shown, can lead to the deterioration of the nervous system, which may in turn result in physical disabilities.

Avoiding Psychological Inducers of Stress

Psychological stress inducers are situations that cause you to worry, get angry, panic, overreact or lose sleep.

These stressors, so-called hot buttons, are different for everyone, but generally they come in two types:

- *Unavoidable Stressors*
These are events that cause profound disquietude—the death of a loved one, a divorce, the loss of a job, an increase in financial obligations, a chronic illness, or an injury. There is often nothing you can do to prevent these stressors.
- *Avoidable Stressors*
These are stressors you can avoid. *You can avoid rushing,* such as not waiting until the last minute to run to the airport, not being late for an appointment, not delaying studying for an exam (you don't want to have to pull an all-nighter), and not procrastinating about work projects.

    You can avoid high-risk situations, such as gambling, or investing in stock market shares or business ventures that you don't fully understand.

    You can shun irritating situations, such as rush-hour traffic or long lines in stores.

    In other words, stop any action that leads you to feel stressed or hurried.

Avoiding Physical Inducers of Stress

Try following these tips in order to avoid self-induced physical stress.

- *Consume Little or No Caffeine*
Although caffeine has some health benefits, it can also lead to anxiety, poor sleep quality, stress, and hand tremors. If you're sensitive to coffee, try decaffeinated coffee or herbal teas instead.
- *Consume Little or No Alcohol*
Although occasionally drinking red wine has been linked to some health benefits, long-term frequent alcohol consumption may lead to mild symptoms of brain and central nervous system deceleration, such as confusion, loss of motor control, body tremors, and behavioral changes.
- *Avoid Recreational Drugs*
Although some recreational drugs are legal, their safety record is still in dispute.
- *Get a Good Night's Sleep*

Adequate sleep means a continuous deep sleep for seven to eight hours per night.

Our obsession with smartphones, social media, TV, and the internet has caused an epidemic of sleep deprivation.

If you don't fall asleep within half an hour of your desired bedtime, try eliminating caffeine, taking a hot shower in the evening, taking natural sleep-promoting supplements, sleeping in a very dark room, and reading a calming book.

Wedding Rings and Health

Does marriage, or a long-term relationship, come with health benefits?

There are numerous studies suggesting that marriage enhances good health and boosts an overall sense of well-being. Harvard University researchers have found that unmarried people are more likely than their married counterparts to contract many types of cancer, such as prostate, lung, and colorectal.

And a study from New York University concluded that married people under the age of fifty have a 12 percent less chance of suffering from cardiovascular disease than unwed individuals.

Marriage also seems to promote longevity. "Being married is a big factor in survivorship," concluded Peter Martin, a professor of human development and family studies at Iowa State University.

What's behind all these benefits?

Is it the social support? Most probably. Companionship—simply not being alone—enhances happiness and therefore health.

Is it intimate relations? That could be a factor. According to a study conducted by the New England Research Institutes, regular sexual activity may lower the risk of heart attacks and strokes in men.

On the other hand, an unhappy marriage or an unhappy long-term relationship can be problematic for your physical and mental health.

A research published in the *Journal of Happiness Studies* states, "Not all marriages are equal: unhappy marriages provide fewer benefits than happy ones. Compared to individuals who were 'very happily' married, those who were 'not too happy' in marriage were over twice as likely to report worse health."

So, the wise choice seems to be: a *happy marriage, or a happy long-term relationship—or none!*

And whether you're married or a in a long-term relationship, or you're not, never were, no longer are or never will be, the most important thing is to remain socially connected.

I will come back to that soon.

My Kidney Chronicle

As I've said, in order to guard our health and well-being, our first duty is to take measures for the prevention and early detection of disease.

Over the years, I've been following my own prevention and early detection rules. I have a yearly physical exam that includes a battery of blood tests. And for early cancer detection, I undergo a full-body screening every few years, in the form of safe X-rays, such as MRIs and ultrasounds. As well, I have regular endoscopies to monitor my gastro-intestinal system.

One year, after I had finished my usual array of blood tests and X-rays, I received a call from a colleague at the radiology clinic where the tests had been done. Dr. Stewart, a gifted radiologist, asked me to meet with him personally. I thought he might have wanted to refer an important patient to my practice. It didn't occur to me that it was related to my testing.

As I entered his office, Dr. Stewart, in contrast to his usual cheerful demeanor, looked dour. He informed me that he had bad news for me: he had just discovered a very large mass, almost the size of a small watermelon, in my left kidney. *And it looked like cancer.*

My whole life turned upside down in mere seconds.

I was in disbelief. This came totally out of the blue. I suddenly saw my days coming to an end. I felt devastated that I would shortly be leaving Stephanie and our two small children behind.

Later that day, however, I composed myself and decided to think rationally.

There was no question about it: I had a large cancerous mass on my kidney, and I needed to act quickly. I went to a prominent urologist I knew for his opinion. He confirmed that there was, as he put it, a 99 percent chance that I had kidney cancer. His conclusion was that major surgery was needed to remove the tumor, as well as the entire kidney around it, as a precautionary measure.

I had a life-altering decision to make. But then I remembered two dictums of mine that aren't yet among my universal rules!

The first is, as I told my TV star patient Denise:

"Different good doctors may offer ... *different good* opinions."

The other one is:

"Of all the big experts I know ... *common sense* **is the biggest!"**

In other words, I needed to consider both the expert knowledge and my common sense. Though I trusted and respected my urologist colleague, I came to the conclusion that, for peace of mind, I should get a second opinion. After I completed my research, I ended up making an appointment with a reputable urologist who specialized in kidney surgery at the Cleveland Clinic.

A week later, I met with Dr. Newman. He was a quiet man of few words. As he reviewed all the test results in his office, I was sitting in front of him with Stephanie, anxiously awaiting his opinion. And honestly, I was expecting that he would come to the same conclusion as the previous urologist.

When he finished his evaluation, he looked at me and said something I will never forget, "I'm not 100 percent sure of what's going on."

Huh? This was an extraordinary comment from a surgeon as competent as he was. Most surgeons are usually very confident in their conclusions.

Dr. Newman continued, "There's something that doesn't click here."

Bewildered, I asked him, "What is it?"

"I'm not sure," he replied. "There's something unusual about your case. Yes, it's probably cancer, but I'm not fully convinced yet. You have got a very large tumor but no symptoms. It sure looks like a cancerous mass, but it may be—I repeat, may be—an unusual type of benign tumor. This possibility, however, is no more than 7 percent likely."

Then Dr. Newman paused for a few seconds before he continues, "If I am the one to operate on you, I won't come up with a plan beforehand. I will make it during the surgery. I will open your abdomen and have a look first before touching anything. And then, based on what I find, I will proceed one step at a time. If this is cancer, I will have to make sure that I won't spread it by going too fast."

His speech was music to my ears. *This man is a thinker*, I thought to myself. I liked his approach. My instinct told me that I could trust him.

Dr. Newman then said, "Please take your time to think about it and let me know. In any case, I will be traveling to Brazil in two weeks for a conference. When I'm back, you can contact me if you're still interested in my being your surgeon."

I interrupted him. "Dr. Newman, I've made up my mind. You're my surgeon!"

He seemed pleased to hear that.

Then, following my Rule 2 (*Ask Once for What You Want*), I continued, "I would really like you to operate on me before you leave for Brazil!"

Surprised by my request, he hesitated for a second, and then briskly said, with a little smile, "Okay. I will do it!"

A few days later, I had my surgery. And guess what? My humongous tumor was *benign!* And just as important, my left kidney was saved.

So, I was both lucky and wise.

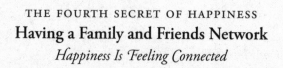

THE FOURTH SECRET OF HAPPINESS
Having a Family and Friends Network
Happiness Is Feeling Connected

The "Social Animal" Phenomenon

Your friends get your jokes. Your family loves you unconditionally. Your coworkers offer you validation. Your spouse hugs you daily. And your kids warm your heart.

Family and friends lift you up when you're down and celebrate with you when you're successful. They provide comfort and have a positive influence on your overall mood.

Everyone in your life collectively boosts your happiness and well-being while decreasing your stress. Why? Because you and I and all of us are *social animals*.

> **We crave to belong—to feel supported and loved.**

Social connectedness boosts physical and mental health. It reinforces emotional well-being, lowers our levels of anxiety, increases our self-esteem, strengthens our immune systems, and boosts longevity.

Conversely, loneliness has been shown to lead to high blood pressure, heart attacks, strokes, drug abuse, alcoholism, and depression. Studies have revealed that a lack of connection is as great a risk factor for early death as smoking fifteen cigarettes a day.

> **Loneliness is a silent killer.**

A Jail Cell, but the Gate Is Unlocked

Think of loneliness as a type of solitary confinement. It's like being in a high-security prison cell, but the door is open!

> **A key to happiness—is not to be alone.**

Happiness is communicating with people, those we care about and those who care about us. We need to socialize with others. We long to express ourselves and listen as others express themselves.

This can be in the form of any communicative exchange—a meeting, a phone call, a video chat, an e-mail—or in person, while watching a movie, playing a team sport, or enjoying a candlelit dinner. Any and all of these qualify as enriching social connections.

Intimate Networks

Family and friends are essential to our happiness.

With them, we know that we're not alone. They offer us comfort and have a positive influence on our overall mood. They keep us calm and quash our stress. They help us manage work and health issues.

Our intimate "F & F" networks, in order of priority, are:
- *The Nuclear Family*
  Including our partners and children.
- *Other Family Members*
  Including parents, grandparents, siblings, cousins, uncles, and aunts.
- *Friends*
  Including close confidants, as well as colleagues and acquaintances.

Some of us care only for our closest friends, our BFFs, and tend to ignore others. That's a mistake.

The reason is what I call the friendship bar.

For close friends, the bar is quite high. They are the ones we know very well—heart to heart. They need to have very good chemistry with us and be 100 percent trustworthy. These are two absolute musts. But those dear individuals are rare. If we have two or three of them, we're very lucky.

For good friends, the bar is in the middle. They need to have a good chemistry with us and be trustworthy. They also must be likable and interesting.

For the acquaintance category, the bar is set low. They only need to be good recreational companions. We don't ask or expect much of acquaintances—just being fun to spend time with is enough, and good occasional company is sufficient.

But the truth is that all kinds of friends can enrich our lives. We just need to be clear about our expectations of them and theirs of us.

They Are Watching Our Watch

Busy though we may be, we must invest in socializing on a daily basis to create and maintain our happiness.

> **Family and friends primarily want one thing from us—our time!**

Fortunately, we are blessed with multiple simple communication platforms that enable us to keep in touch, including the phone, text messages, e-mails, and video chats. And even though technology is fantastic when we are pressed for time or separated by geographic distance, the old-fashioned, in-person, face-to-face gathering is still best of all.

No matter what method you choose, the important thing is to connect regularly with family members and friends.

So:

> **Block off 5 minutes daily—for family and friends bonding.**

Ideally, use those minutes to make a quick phone call to one of the people in your networks. Even if you keep the conversation short, the link is strengthened. Something as simple as a one-line text or an e-mail asking, "How are you?" or saying "Hope all is well" can nourish your family and friends "F & F" loop.

Later, when you have time, you can arrange to meet in person—the ultimate connection.

It's the Loop That Matters

Just knowing that there are people out there who care for you is what's important.

> The value of the "F & F" loop is in its ... mere existence.

It's like having a mother who lives in a city far from you. Even if you see her only once a year, you know she is there to provide you with love and support, and that's enough to contribute to your happiness.

Finally, if you're short on family and friends, create an alternative loop by joining an activity group, such as a club, an association, a class or a recreational gathering. There are tons of opportunities for connection available through the internet. And there are plenty of people on the planet who could add to your happiness. You just need to meet them halfway.

RULE 10

in a Pearl Shell

Your #1 Goal in Life Is Happiness
*How to Implement the Four Indispensable Secrets
of Living Happily*

THE FIRST SECRET OF HAPPINESS
Working and Keeping Busy

Happiness Isn't *Owning* Things ... but *Doing* Things!

- No Object—Once Obtained—Can Keep You Perpetually Entertained
- What's Important Isn't Owning Things, But Doing Things
- You Need Something to Get Up for Every Morning
- Keep Working, Keep Busy
- The Harder You Work During the Week, the More You Enjoy Your Weekend!

THE SECOND SECRET OF HAPPINESS
Having Exciting Expectations

Happiness Is the Yellow Brick Road to the Exciting *Goal* ... That Ends Once You Reach That *Goal*!

- Thrilling Expectations Give You Something to Look for in the Future
- Like Dorothy's Enchanted Trip, Happiness Is the Yellow Brick Road to the Exciting Goal
  But Once You Reach That Goal ... You Need to Find Another Exciting One
- Your Life Should Be a Succession of Exciting Goals

RULE 10

in a Pearl Shell

THE THIRD SECRET OF HAPPINESS
Staying Healthy
The Crucial Steps for *Prevention and Early Detection*
of Cancer, Heart Disease, Diabetes, and Alzheimer's Disease
- If You're Sick, It's Difficult to Be Happy
- Stay Healthy Both Physically and Psychologically
- The Best Cure of All Is Prevention and Early Detection
- Check with Your Physician First, and With Your Common Sense Second

THE FOURTH SECRET OF HAPPINESS
Having a *Family and Friends* Network
Happiness Is *Feeling Connected*
- Loneliness Is a Silent Killer
- We Crave to Belong and Be Loved
- Family and Friends Want One Thing from You: Your Time Block Off 5 Minutes Daily for Them

WHEN YOU DON'T KNOW WHAT TO DO ... DO NOTHING!

Time Will Often Reveal the Solution

The "Don't Just Sit There" Phenomenon

Parents sometimes criticize their children for not doing anything on a sunny Saturday. They will say something such as, "Don't just sit there—*do* something!"

The idea is that doing anything is better than doing nothing.

As adults, we still feel compelled to keep busy all the time—to do something. We live in a high-tech culture of instant decision making and fast reactions. We are quick to pick up the phone or press the *Send* button, often without thinking things through.

But how often, afterward, do we tell ourselves, *I wish I hadn't done that?* This compulsion to do something can be problematic.

The "Do Just Sit There" Phenomenon

There are times, however, when we are seemingly unable to take action and incapable of making a choice.

We become stuck in our ambivalence as we ponder various scenarios, slowed down by the prospect of making the wrong decision. We just can't pull the trigger, because we don't know which target that bullet should be hitting. Faced with multiple competing scenarios, we're unable to reach a decision and choose among the options.

Our natural reaction, then, is to feel pressured, to feel the compulsion to *do something.* And if, finally, we force ourselves to act, and we make a decision and do something, we may still end up wishing we had waited longer. A decision made in haste often backfires.

Therefore, when hesitating between options, don't be pressured by yourself or anyone else to act.

You owe no actions ... to anyone.

In such an unsure predicament:

**Hesitating between multiple options—
is enough reason ... not to act on any!**

In such a case, what you need to do first is follow Rule 8: *Put Your Problems on Paper.* Start by comparing your options—in writing.

If you do so and you're still hesitating, it simply means that *no option is good enough.*

In that case, your best plan of action is to:

Do nothing—just wait!

Let time give you the answer.

Before the Final Act, an Intermission Is in Order

Time often works magic at clearing up confusion and recasting matters in a different light.

As time passes, your options either:

Lose steam—and get downgraded in importance, or gain momentum—and get upgraded.

Consider the situation of Samantha. She is a lady in her late thirties who dreams of getting married and having children. She receives a marriage proposal and feels it may be the answer to her dreams, but she isn't sure whether or not to accept it. *She hesitates.*

Perhaps she imagines that there may be somebody out there who is better. Or maybe she isn't convinced that her suitor is an appropriate husband. Or maybe she just doesn't feel enough passion for him.

On the one hand, Samantha doesn't seem excited about accepting this man's proposal. But on the other hand, she is flattered by it and worried that it could be her last chance to say "Yes" to a good person who is down on his knee before her. *She hesitates.*

What does this hesitation mean?

> **Hesitation is the unsettled score**
> **—of the battle between—**
> **the positive and negative aspects of a situation.**

To Samantha, it means that the potential joys of getting married and having children (the positive aspect) are neutralized by a lack of enthusiasm for merging her life with that of her suitor (the negative aspect).

Thinking about her options and discussing the situation with a parent or a best friend may help Samantha clarify her feelings. However, forcing herself to make a decision or act on other people's advice isn't only a bad idea, but can also be downright harmful if it causes her, against her instincts, to either accept or reject the proposal. *Therefore, the wisest thing for Samantha to do is pause and wait.*

Meanwhile, she could, of course, keep her options open. She could conceivably inform her suitor that she is seriously thinking about his proposal and needs some time to make up her mind, which are all true.

New developments often come up. Perceptions and feelings constantly change.

> **Sooner or later,**
> **time will upgrade the right option.**

It did for Samantha. A few weeks later, she made up her mind to kindly reject the proposal. Luckily, she met the right person for her almost four years later and accepted to tie the knot, this time with no hesitation whatsoever.

So, in business, romance, or relationships:

> **If you feel hesitant—**
> **take your time . . . before taking action.**

Beverly Hills Blues

About twenty years ago, at an annual meeting of the American Academy of Facial Plastic and Reconstructive Surgery in Los Angeles, I presented a talk on a technique I had developed and written about called Lip Lift, an innovative procedure to improve the appearance of aging lips.

After my lecture, Dr. Bastock, a renowned plastic surgeon practicing in Beverly Hills, approached me to say that he was interested in watching my technique. He asked if he could visit my operating room in Montreal, and I said yes.

Two months later, Dr. Bastock arrived to witness the surgery, as well as a series of other cosmetic procedures. He seemed attentive, asking many questions as he observed me.

At the end of the surgical day, Dr. Bastock insisted on taking me out for dinner. We went to an exquisite French restaurant, Bonaparte, in old Montreal. Over wine and a delicious meal, Dr. Bastock thanked me for the day. Then he added a surprise: he invited me to join his Beverly Hills practice as a partner!

He thought that since I performed a number of unique techniques, such as some mini-incision procedures, combining our skills would be beneficial both to his practice and mine. I was taken by surprise. I didn't see that coming. I promised Dr. Bastock that I would consider his offer.

At home that evening, I discussed it with my wife, Stephanie. I told her that I was torn between two competing options.

One was to join an established practice in the most glamorous destination for plastic surgery in the United States. This would ultimately enhance my career, my income, and my reputation.

The other was to stay in Montreal, a pleasant bilingual city with a European flair, where I felt completely at home, and where my two little children were very happy at their schools. My parents and my brother, Sam, an established and respected ophthalmologist, also lived in Montreal. In addition, Stephanie and I had a large group of good friends in the city. I also had a popular clinic in Westmount, an elegant Montreal suburb, complete with a panoramic view of Mount Royal, a beautiful mountain. And I was very fortunate to have a home right on a lake, just a twenty-minute drive from downtown.

Making this decision was difficult. I was very conflicted about it. I didn't know what to do.

Dr. Bastock soon called and invited Stephanie and I to spend three days at his Los Angeles home to get a feel for his city. We gladly accepted.

The stay in Beverly Hills was surreal. We were surrounded by elegance, wealth, superb weather, and friendly people. Dr. Bastock's office, on Sunset Boulevard, one of many plastic surgery clinics in the building, was as impressive as his house. And Dr. Bastock was a gentleman who was pleasant and generous throughout our stay.

At the end of our visit, I asked Dr. Bastock to give me some more time to think over his offer. He agreed. The pressure was mounting.

When we returned to Montreal, Stephanie informed me that she would leave the final decision to me. Then, I was really stuck. I still didn't know what to do.

Over the following few months, and after many discussions and hesitations, I finally concluded that the change in the physical and social environment of our lives would be much too chaotic for us. I therefore came to the decision to respectfully decline Dr. Bastock 's offer, who has since remained a good friend.

Looking back, I now realize that I agonized for almost a year for nothing. Back then, I hadn't discovered the rule I'm giving you here. If I had, as soon as I felt that I didn't know what to do, I would have done nothing—just waited, without all that anxiety. That would have allowed time to guide me to the right solution.

I was lucky, in a way, that I didn't hurry into committing myself, under pressure, to one option or the other, either by following other people's advice or my own impulses. Making a choice just because you feel you have to is a grave mistake.

When in doubt, you should wait. In such cases, waiting and doing nothing are the right actions.

RULE 11

in a Pearl Shell

When You Don't Know What to Do ...
Do Nothing!
Time Will Often Reveal the Solution

- When Hesitating Between Multiple Options,
  Do Nothing—and Wait
- Sooner or Later, *Time Will Upgrade the Right Option*
- And Don't Allow Yourself to Be Rushed
  You Owe No Actions ... to Anyone

WHEN YOU DON'T KNOW WHAT TO SAY ...
SAY NOTHING!

Silence Is Often Your Best Reply

The "Say Something" Phenomenon

Throughout our daily lives, one interaction after another seems to require a verbal response. No matter who is asking a question or making a statement, it may feel as if you have to respond.

Silence is awkward.

As a result, you may rush to fill it. But should you?

We all face unpleasant and uncomfortable situations that destabilize us and may even anguish us. Opinions and comments leap at us at a rapid pace throughout the day. At any given point, we may be challenged on our points of view, our political inclinations, our behavior, our performance, or virtually anything we say or do—even on what we don't say or do.

For example, you might be told a vulgar joke that repulses you and be expected to laugh. You might overhear a prejudicial comment that truly offends you. You could be wrongly criticized by a colleague, or verbally abused by a customer, or asked for a favor that you don't feel comfortable doing. Or you could be intimidated into buying something, saying something, or agreeing to something that you would prefer not to buy, say, or agree to.

At all such moments, on top of being agitated, you will most likely feel compelled to respond—to say something. It's human nature.

A Fight or Flight—or a Dive

In all such emotionally taxing situations, you might feel angry, anxious, embarrassed, resentful, threatened, or insulted.

At these fight or flight moments, you may often feel the urge to speak.

Your stress level shoots up exponentially, while your brain races to find an ideal reply. A hundred thoughts rush through your mind, as you attempt to strike a right-this-second appropriate reaction: Should you agree or disagree? Should you attack or apologize?

In such instances, when your back is up against the wall, you feel the need to come up with an instant response.

Well, you're wrong.

You owe no instant responses . . . to anyone.

But what should you do when facing one of these challenging situations?

If a response comes naturally to you, without effort, stress or hesitation, then great—say it. But if you're uncomfortable or unsure, your best course of action is to resist the urge to talk.

Just dive into silence.

"Silence is sometimes the best answer," said the Dalai Lama (when he wasn't silent!).

By staying quiet and composed, you put your opponent off balance. You instantly gain the upper hand.

And if the person you're talking to pressures you to say something, just reply:

"I'll think about it."

And if the question is repeated, keep repeating the same response, "I'll think about it."

And you don't have to react physically either.

**If you don't feel like smiling or laughing, don't—
just maintain a neutral, relaxed expression.**

The "Undeliberatable" Story

Susie, a competent and loyal head nurse at my surgical center, once asked to meet me in private to discuss a matter related to her nursing team, a group of eight highly skilled nurses.

As she sat opposite me in my office at the end of a long surgical day, she wore a serious expression. "We have a problem," she stated. "Two of the nurses are complaining that you often finish operating too late in the day."

I was taken aback—and a little annoyed. I thought that being so busy in the operating room would make these two nurses happy rather than upset, since they were both being paid by the hour. I also had a suspicion that this complaint may have been a disguised attempt to get a raise. In such a case, I would be doubly disappointed that the complaining nurses didn't appreciate the fact that they were paid well above market rate as it was.

Knowing Susie, I was sure that she wasn't on the side of the nurses complaining about the late surgical schedule. I also had no intention of reducing the number of my surgeries or raising my already high pay rate before the end of the year.

In other words, I didn't feel like arguing the obvious, or defending the defensible. And I wasn't in the mood of deliberating over the undeliberatable!

I didn't know what to say, so I just said nothing.

After a few seconds, Susie relaunched the discussion. "What do you think, Doctor?"

Still, I said nothing.

Susie, one smart-cookie messenger, got the message. As she stood to leave, she said, "I will solve it. Don't worry, Doctor."

I wasn't worried at all. And I was pleased that the problem was solved so smoothly—and so silently!

Stop, and Let the "Taboo Trio" Pass

At a medical conference in Miami three years ago, I was out for drinks with a group of doctors. The majority of them were barely acquaintances, much less friends.

At one point during the evening, the subject of the American presidency and the two main governing parties came up. You can just imagine the flurry of controversial opinions that erupted. There were supporters and detractors on both sides, with the consumption of alcohol fueling the heated discourse. I felt as if I was walking into a trap: *anything you say could be used against you!*

The same thing could have happened if we had been talking about any controversial topic, such as global warming, religion, gender equality, abortion, immigration, or racial stereotypes. These are fine subjects to discuss among family and close friends, but they turn into no-win topics when you're interacting with people you hardly know.

So, when you're among strangers, and if a discussion comes up that touches on the three "touchy untouchable" subjects of:

The "Taboo Trio"—*sex, religion, and politics.*

In such confrontations: *Just listen—don't talk.*

Saying nothing is often your best strategy. Silence is so much better than the alternatives—argument, attack, and defense. Instead of getting stressed in a no-win situation, you can sit happily back, relax, and take stock of what other people are saying.

There is power in saying . . . nothing!

RULE 12

in a Pearl Shell

When You Don't Know What to Say ...
Say Nothing!
Silence Is Often Your Best Reply

- *Silence Is Awkward*
- If You're Struggling to Respond, *Dive into Silence*
- *You Owe No Answers ... to Anyone*
- If Pressed, Say, *"I'll Think About It."*
- *If You Don't Feel Like Smiling, Don't*
- And Let the *Taboo Trio* Pass: *Sex, Religion, and Politics*
- *There Is Power in Saying Nothing*

DON'T GAMBLE WITH WHAT YOU CAN'T AFFORD TO LOSE

Luck Is Fickle

The "All or Nothing" Phenomenon

Meet Bruno, an office clerk on a tight monthly budget of $3,000.

On the first day of the month, unable to pay all his bills, he decides to visit a local casino. He tells himself that he is a good player and that he has a decent chance of doubling or tripling his money. And if he does win, all his problems will be solved. Overcome with excitement and hope, he gambles it all—the entire $3,000.

Regardless of whether he loses that money or doubles it, I have a question for you: What's your view of Bruno's master plan? You probably think the guy is nuts. It's true that if he wins, he wins it all. But if he loses, he loses everything, and there is no turning back. It's an all-or-nothing hazard—too much of a gamble.

Yet, haven't we all at some point taken too much of a gamble, an unwise risk for an irresistible potential reward? We hope against hope that luck will be in our favor, even when it's most unlikely. When chasing a desperate prospect, craving for an alluring gain, or itching for a seductive experience, we may be very tempted to take huge chances, ones that will yield catastrophic results should we lose. Yet we take them anyway.

Not Coming Back, but Please Call Back

This is a not-so-uncommon story.

Sara, a respected employee in a successful Wall Street company, feels she isn't fairly compensated for her talent and asks her boss for a significant raise. She is told politely to be patient and that the company will take the matter under consideration the following year.

However, in a fit of defiance, and feeling irreplaceable, she submits her resignation, convinced that her company will panic, rush to call her back, and accept her ultimatum.

Unfortunately for her, though, that call never comes. Distraught, she contacts the firm to tell them that she has changed her mind. But the company won't change its mind!

This is a perfect illustration of the adage "Don't burn your bridges behind you." That's exactly what Sara did. She burned her most important bridge. Rather than being flexible and patient, she became irrational and arrogant, all to her detriment. Sadly, she lost her lucrative job.

She simply gambled with something that she couldn't afford to lose.

I Love You, and Others

Here is another not-so-uncommon story.

Arthur, a businessman with a great job, a loving wife, and two young children, seems to have the perfect life. He should be content, shouldn't he?

Well, not exactly, according to him. While traveling for work, he frequently gets the chance to socialize with attractive women and occasionally strays from his marriage. These dalliances become more frequent as his pleasurable conquests expand.

Since he gets away with those early exploits, he gains the confidence to repeat his deceitful actions. The more he does it, the more emboldened he becomes. As professional poker player Terrence "VP Pappy" Murphy observed, "A gambler never makes the same mistake twice. It's usually three or more times!"

Unfortunately for Arthur, one of his regular girlfriends finds his home phone number and starts harassing him. Worse, she files a paternity suit against him, claiming that she is pregnant and he is the father.

What began as a mere lark has turned into an unmitigated disaster. Predictably, Arthur's wife finds out about the affair. At that point, it's far too late for Arthur to repair the situation. No apology will do, and his marriage is ruined.

All this because Arthur gambled with something he couldn't afford to lose.

The "Too Smart" Phenomenon

Arthur's and Sara's stories are among thousands of similar tragedies. People follow their impulses and gamble away relationships, jobs, and possessions that they can't afford to lose.

Why? Because they feel they're *smart enough to win and shrewd enough not to lose.*

Unfortunately, as writer Brandon Mull noted, "Luck has a way of evaporating when you lean on it!"

When you roll the dice:

> You never know when you will get . . .
> the *combination of numbers* that you least expect!
> And if your luck goes south—you lose and are lost!

To Be or Not to Be . . . Chancing It

Soon after Stephanie and I married, we started looking for a new place to call home.

Our dream was to one day build a house directly on the water. But as you can imagine, vacant waterfront lots close to downtown Montreal were quite expensive. Refusing to relinquish our dream, we continued looking into pricey waterfront homes and lots.

We finally came across a beautiful and very spacious half-acre parcel that had just recently been placed on the market. It was a rare find. The lot was great, but its price was even greater! So, I informed the real estate agent that I loved the land but couldn't afford it.

However, sometimes in life, some of us get a lucky break. And our turn had just arrived.

Unexpectedly, the real estate market entered into a recession. The precious piece of land started to decline in value. By the time the real estate agent called us back, it was already down 20 percent from its original price.

Since I didn't have much to lose, I decided to take my chances and just wait it out while watching the market carefully. I knew that prices could fluctuate, but I also knew I would still have time to adjust.

The price kept going down, and I kept waiting. Finally, when I felt the market was going to reverse its course, I made my move and bought the land at 40 percent of its original price.

My risk was acceptable. I took the gamble because I could afford to lose.

Now for another story of mine.

The prestigious building in which my clinic is housed is a modern classic designed by the renowned architect Ludwig Mies van der Rohe. My clinic, taking almost half of a high floor, has a wonderful view of Montreal. I also have access to indoor parking and to my own reserved table at a nice restaurant in the building called Tavern on the Square. In short, everything about the location is ideal.

One year, when it was time to renew my lease, the landlord presented me with an offer that I thought was reasonably good. But following my own Rule 2—*Ask Once for What You Want*—I requested a better deal!

The landlord's answer came back negative. In addition, the building manager informed me that if the lease wasn't signed by the end of the week, the landlord wouldn't honor the offer and would put my space on the market.

I had a major decision to make. Should I gamble and insist on a sweeter deal? With an office space as large as mine, I knew that finding another space with similar amenities wouldn't be easy. However, I also felt that both the landlord and his manager were probably bluffing.

Yet, bluffing or not, the important question for me was: Could I take a chance on losing these premises? I knew I wouldn't have had enough time to find another space, much less fully rebuild my operating room and move all the equipment and furniture, before the landlord would want me out of the building if he found another tenant.

I couldn't take a chance; I couldn't gamble with what I couldn't afford to lose.

So, I signed the lease!

The Casino's Secret Formula

Casinos know that their fortunes depend on this secret: The more gamblers win, the more they trust their good luck, and the more they continue playing—until they lose everything.

Never gamble with an asset *you can't afford to lose*.

Whether your risk involves money, a job, a relationship, or your health, don't follow your impulses or overestimate your abilities.

When the stakes are high, don't rely on luck.

Don't step inside the . . . casino of life.

Sooner or later, your luck will run out.

And sooner or later, the dice will deliver the least expected numbers . . . and lightning will strike.

In the casino of life, as in the neighborhood casino:

The house always wins—not you!

Unaffordable Bet, Indecent Backlash

Remember the movie *Indecent Proposal,* starring Demi Moore, Woody Harrelson, and Robert Redford?

Moore is happily married to Harrelson, but the couple has no money. So, they go to a casino in hopes of a turnaround. And it's there that a billionaire, played by Redford, comes along and offers the couple $1 million if Moore would sleep with him for just one night.

The couple risks it all. They figure that one night of infidelity will be a fleeting trifle that will make no difference to their marriage, whereas the money will be a durable fortune.

Unfortunately for them, they were unaware of this favorite quotation, "Life is like a gamble. Sometimes you win; sometimes you lose. But whatever cards you play in life, whether club, spade, or diamond, always remember, never play with the heart!"

They played with the heart. They should have known that a happy marriage is an invaluable bond that they couldn't afford to lose. But they still went ahead and staked it.

And the result was the disintegration of their marriage—and their dignity.

RULE 13

in a Pearl Shell

Don't Gamble with What You Can't Afford to Lose
Luck Is Fickle

- *Don't Trust Your Luck or Your Intelligence*
  Never Gamble with an Asset Crucial to You
- In the Casino of Life, as in the Neighborhood Casino:
  The House Always Wins—Not You!
- *In Gambling, Sooner or Later, Lightning Will Strike!*
  The Dice Will Deliver the *Least Expected Numbers,* and
  Then . . . You Lose and Are Lost!

THAT SINKING FEELING INSIDE MEANS—STOP

That Four-Million-Year-Old Alarm System Within Us

Sinking Means Thinking

Have you ever been in a situation that triggered immediate discomfort? Like a knot in your stomach? Like a sinking feeling inside? And you intuitively knew that something was wrong?

We are all born with a four-million-year-old inner instinctive mechanism. It's an inbred sensory device that magically forewarns us to invisible threats. This mechanism was bequeathed to us by our ancestors, who regularly accumulated experiences in facing all kinds of environmental hazards.

It's like an antenna implanted deep within our psyches, dormant but ready to spring into action and alert us to danger. It's a blessing.

Fast-forward to the twenty-first century, and it's still there, as invaluable as ever.

And this alarm system is further fine-tuned by our own past and present individual experiences, as well as by the knowledge we compile throughout life.

So, whenever you feel that unpleasant feeling in your stomach, remind yourself that this is nature's way of giving you a warning that danger lies just ahead. And more often than not, it's correct.

When you sense that something is off, pay very special attention to that hunch. Trust it.

For example, if you're in the midst of making an important decision dealing with a potential business partner, a date, or even a family member or a spouse, be on the lookout for that distressing feeling, warning you that something is wrong.

It's telling you to:

> **Stop—right now.**

You absolutely must listen to it and go into a pause mode. You need to start thinking why you feel the way you do.

In other words:

> When you start sinking . . . start thinking!

From Warm to Lukewarm, That's Trouble

As the CEO of a Canadian company, Joe, whom I met and befriended on a South American cruise a few years ago, had increased the corporation's profits by more than 200 percent over a period of just four years. He had reason to celebrate.

The problem, however, was that he worked for a family-owned business—and he wasn't a member of the family. Though he was warmly treated by the French owners and felt reasonably secure in his job, he always had this shadowy feeling hanging over him, that a young, ambitious family member would one day be groomed to usurp his position.

Joe recounted to me that, one day, at the annual board meeting, he walked toward his usual seat at the table. The attendees were looking down at their agendas as usual. Each board member wore a neutral expression. Nothing seemed to be obviously wrong.

But Joe told me that he had a bad feeling all of a sudden. From the second he stepped into the room, he immediately sensed something wasn't right. He had that sinking feeling inside. He became perturbed and uneasy, sensing that his job was threatened. He wondered if the board was planning to replace him with a family member. Although he started sweating a bit, he hid it.

As he sat down, he calmly opened his notes to begin the meeting, but the wheels in his head kept spinning. He immediately conjured a delaying strategy. He introduced some details to his report that complicated the big picture and somewhat disarmed the board, which ended up keeping the status quo. He thought he averted the threat of dismissal, but he felt it was a close call.

Joe proceeded immediately to look for a position elsewhere while still monitoring the situation at his workplace carefully. The lukewarm reception he had been receiving lately from the company's owners confirmed his suspicions.

A month later, he had an exciting offer from another American company. Before accepting it, he figured that the decent thing to do was at least to have a discussion with his present employer. He told his boss that his wife, a nurse, had a job offer in the United States and that he was thinking of following her for a year or two. The owner seemed relieved to hear that and encouraged Joe to join his wife and to leave as quickly as he wished.

Joe told me that he accepted the new job offer immediately and thanked his lucky stars—and his subconscious instinct. And then he added with a grin, "Nabil, it's always easier to get a job when one is employed than when one isn't!"

Spanish Treachery

Around four years ago, Beatrice, one of my clinic assistants, decided to spend her three-week summer vacation in Europe. Her family was originally from France, and she wanted to meet her French relatives.

Beatrice, a smart young woman in her late twenties, had been working for me for two years. She was quiet and pleasant. She was also highly intelligent and resourceful, which motivated me to give her a raise within her first six months.

On her last day of work before vacation, Beatrice came to say good-bye to me. I wished her a safe journey and a good time in France. But as she left my office, I had an uneasy feeling about our farewell, an unsettling discomfort. Something about it just didn't feel right. I had that sinking feeling inside.

The next morning, I shared my suspicions with Nirvana, the office manager. She dismissed my concern and reassured me that Beatrice loved her job and would be back. "Why would she leave such a good job for another one that won't be easy to find?" she reasoned. I agreed with her rationale. Knowing how shrewd Nirvana was, I convinced myself that whatever I felt had no factual basis and told myself to forget about it.

But that stubborn, unsettling feeling wouldn't let go. Two days later, I reopened the discussion with Nirvana. This time, I asked her to start looking for a new assistant. I told her that if Beatrice did come back, we could always call off our search. Nirvana felt it was a waste of time, but did as I asked and started looking for replacements. She ended up meeting two good potential candidates.

The day before Beatrice was expected back, I again discussed the situation with Nirvana. I told her that I had probably exaggerated my feelings and that Beatrice would likely show up. She reassured me that she would.

The following morning at eight o'clock, Beatrice did not show up for work as usual. And by the end of the day, with Beatrice not returning her calls or e-mails, we both came to the conclusion that she wasn't coming back after all. Later, we learned that she had planned to get engaged in Spain and to continue working there afterward.

Fortunately, one of the two candidates we had already interviewed seemed promising, so we hired her. That new candidate turned out to be excellent and is still working at our clinic.

I always wondered why I had that feeling that didn't make any sense at the time but turned out to be right. Was it the look in Beatrice's eyes? Her tone or body language? I have no idea. But there was something that set off my internal alarm system. And thanks to that instinct, I was able to avert a staffing crisis.

To this day, Nirvana, who is usually very astute, believes that I have a super intuition!

RULE 14

in a Pearl Shell

That Sinking Feeling Inside Means—STOP
That Four-Million-Year-Old Alarm System Within Us

- When You Feel a *Knot in Your Stomach*, It's Telling You: *STOP*—and Watch Out for Trouble
- You Need to *Think* Why You Felt That Way: When You Start *Sinking* . . . Start *Thinking*!

CREATE SMART HABITS THAT SIMPLIFY YOUR LIFE

The Magic of Automated Living

A Habit Sustained Is a Sustained Success

"We are what we repeatedly do. Excellence, therefore, is not an act but a habit," wrote Aristotle in his *Nicomachean Ethics,* as interpreted by Will Durant.

Indeed, all high achievers, be they entrepreneurs, academics, writers, or scientists, have one intriguing thing in common: *a pattern of habits—a specific routine they repeat daily.* Those repeated rituals, some of them bordering on the quirky, seem to be key to keeping their output both sustainable and superior.

Leo Tolstoy, the Russian author, said, "I must write each day without fail, in order not to get out of my routine."

Ludwig van Beethoven, the acclaimed composer, rose at dawn and had only coffee for breakfast, but he made sure to measure sixty beans per cup (talk about a risky energy boost!). By early afternoon, he had already been composing music for several hours.

Haruki Murakami, the Japanese novelist, declared, "The repetition itself becomes the important thing. I get up at 4:00 am and work for five to six hours. In the afternoon, I run for ten kilometers."

Kurt Vonnegut, the American author, woke up at 5:30 a.m. and was obsessed with doing push-ups and sit-ups all day.

W. H. Auden, the American poet, had a routine timed to the minute: meals, writing, hobbies, shopping, and even the mail delivery were all taken into account.

Ingmar Bergman, the Swedish filmmaker, worked eight hours daily—painstaking efforts that often resulted in only three minutes of finished footage.

Benjamin Franklin, one of the founding fathers of the United States, had what he called *air baths* every morning, which meant sitting in front of his open first-floor window naked! He was convinced that this strange ritual was essential to his creativity.

And then there was Darwin.

Charles Darwin, the genius behind the theory of evolution and one of most distinguished creative minds in history, had the most balanced, the most varied, and, above all, the most leisurely and fun-filled of all daily routines.

First thing in the morning, Darwin would take a nice short walk. Then, at 8 a.m., he began ninety minutes of work in his study.

Afterward, another break was due. Lying on the sofa, he would listen to his wife, Emma, read family letters aloud. She would then read excerpts from a novel for him too. At 10:30 a.m., it was time for Darwin to return to his study and resume writing until noon.

After lunch, he answered his letters until around 3 p.m. Then it was time for relaxation again. He would lie on his sofa with a cigarette, while Emma resumed reading the novel. This was followed by half an hour of unwinding in his drawing room, then he had another cigarette while listening to another delightful reading session.

Following a family dinner, he played a game of backgammon and enjoyed even more reading. Then, before bed, Darwin would lie down on his sofa again and listen to Emma—play the piano this time.

A key to Darwin's productivity was that he filled his day with intermittent recreational and pleasant activities. Although he only did three hours of focused work daily, he still managed to produce some of the world's most significant contributions to science.

Figuring Out Which Seat to Sit On

One of my duties as a university professor is to attend a weekly scientific gathering called "grand rounds," in which teachers and surgical residents meet to present, analyze, and exchange views on challenging cases.

At one of these grand rounds, as I walked into the three-hundred-seat university auditorium, I headed directly toward my usual seat, located on the right end of the second row.

In just that moment, I had an epiphany: I noticed that I had unconsciously chosen that same seat, week after week. Why, I wondered? Was I in some way programmed to gravitate toward it?

As I looked around, I realized that every one of the forty attendees, whether a professor or a postgraduate student, was likewise sitting exactly where he or she always does, despite the abundance of empty seats throughout the auditorium.

Obviously, we all shared this predisposition to sit in a familiar place, one to which we had grown accustomed. Without thinking about it, we were in the habit of doing it, which seemed to breed some sort of ease and gave each one of us a sense of familiarity.

That same phenomenon crops up elsewhere in our lives: we choose, time after time, the same parking spot at a shopping center, the same place at the dinner table, and the same side of the bed.

> **We are creatures of habit.**

Why a Habit Becomes a Habit

What are habits, really?

Habits are repeatable automatic actions that are both alluring and comforting to us.

But why is that so? The answer is surprising:

> **Habits allow us to do things—without thinking!**

Habits save us time and stress by reducing the number of decisions we make. We carry out hundreds of habits on a daily basis, from the time we wake up to the time we go to bed. And they help us get through our days easily and efficiently.

A Brain Love Story

But why are habits so addictive?

The beauty of habits is that we don't have to think about them once they're ingrained in our daily routines. When we fall into a habit, we repeatedly follow the same course of action. We don't consciously analyze it. The tedious decision of what to do has been made, so there is no need to make it again.

In other words:

> Habits save us the mental effort—
> of thinking and making decisions.

This fact is welcome news to our brain. After all, it's busy enough—working nonstop, constantly on duty, continuously analyzing, and making choices. It could use a rest every now and then.

Habits allow it to turn off the switch of active thinking and indulge in a passive mode for a change. Whenever we are doing something without thinking about it, like watching a movie, taking a walk, or repeating an automatic action, our brain can relax.

> Habits are addictive to our brains because they are . . . effortless!

And that's why our brains are in love with our habits.

The Tale of "One Nail In, One Nail Out"

Of course, not all habits are created equal. And not all of them are good for us.

Overeating, overdrinking, overspending, smoking, gambling, watching too much TV, and texting while driving are all detrimental habits, sometimes life-threatening ones. They provide temporary pleasure and comfort, a payoff that leaves us feeling good even if what we're doing is bad for us.

Then there are the innocuous habits that aren't dangerous but are nonetheless annoying to other people, such as looking at our phones when somebody is talking to us, habitual clearing of the throat, chewing loudly, sniffling, knee bouncing, talking at the movies, nail biting, or blurting out profanities, to name just a few.

Is there a way to change these less-than-ideal habits into better ones?

It's wishful thinking to believe that a bad habit can be dismantled fully by sheer force of will. It won't work. *It's a rotten deal for the brain to accept.*

This is because our brain favors:

> An *effortless* action—an appealing source of pleasure, over
> A *conscious* action—an unappealing demand for effort.

Therefore, the only way to stop a detrimental habit is to replace it with a habit of a beneficial nature.

> Only an *effortless* good habit
> can overcome an *effortless* bad one.

As the Dutch philosopher Erasmus said, "A nail is driven out by another nail; habit is overcome by habit."

The Three Musketeers of Smart Habits

How can new healthful habits be acquired, nurtured, and kept alive?

Try the following three-pronged approach.

• *Offer a Seductive Deal to Your Brain*

In order to adopt a habit that's sustainable, it has to be reasonably attractive to your brain.

Your brain will promptly reject any bad deal. It will not accept giving up a pleasant routine, such as having a few beers and chips every evening while listening to the news, for an unpleasant experience, such as forcing yourself to resist temptation and instead drink water while chomping on celery sticks.

However, your brain will usually be amenable to a fair compromise: perhaps nonalcoholic beer or some sparkling water with lemon, and fruit combined with low-carb crackers will do the trick. In such a case, your brain will be at least somewhat satisfied. And your waistline will thank you for it.

So, under certain circumstances, your brain will accept losing some of its accustomed indulgences for another routine that provides less but just enough pleasure.

• *Repeat the New Habit*

Repetition works, repetition works!

Like anything in life, whether it's learning a musical instrument, a dance routine or a computer software program, doing something repeatedly produces mastery and automation.

This same principle applies to any new habit.

If you can repeat a task daily for a full month, and if you have established a reasonable substitute that your brain can accept or at least tolerate, then the new behavior will dethrone the old one and will ultimately become a new effortless habit.

In other words, the implementation of smart habits has the primary goal of achieving difficult tasks automatically, through repetition.

The goal is *automation*—but the mechanism is *repetition.*

• *Involve Another Person with Your Habit*

A good strategy for overcoming bad habits is to use the buddy system: calling upon someone else to support your effort.

The idea is to have that person become part of your new routine. Your friend, spouse, or colleague will be there to encourage you and keep you accountable when you're tempted to give up.

Basically:

Your buddy gets into the habit . . . of being part of your habit!

This will give you a support system that will make it easier for you to maintain your new habit.

Norma's Loss Is Her Gain

Norma is a fifty-eight-year-old office manager who was at one time proud of her appearance.

However, her positive self-image turned negative as she began to overeat and gain weight rapidly after the breakup of a long-term relationship. Feeling sad and lonely, she no longer bothered to exercise and began eating ice cream and high-carbohydrate foods for comfort. It wasn't long before she was having trouble fitting into her clothes. That's when she became truly worried.

After reading two diet books and going through many of the weight-loss articles shared on the internet, she attempted a number of crash diets.

Initially, she decided to cut out all bread and potatoes. The first week was agonizing, with cravings driving her crazy. By the tenth day, she reverted to eating bread.

The following week, in a renewed effort, she cut out all desserts. But that resolution, like the previous one, weakened quickly.

Afterward, she followed a regimented diet with detailed instructions for calculating what and how much to eat. Before long, though, she was tired of counting calories and measuring out little portions of food that didn't satisfy her.

Then, she heard about a miraculous prepared meal system. It would be effortless—an easy habit to adopt. All she needed to do was buy the precooked breakfasts, lunches and dinners. It worked amazingly well for a month. However, she eventually became bored with the menu selection and unenthusiastic about ordering more meals.

At that point, she realized she needed to change her approach. She decided to lower her impossibly high expectations for drastic weight loss. *Instead, she would aim for achieving less in order to achieve something.* So, she changed her goal to losing ten pounds instead of forty.

Instead of eliminating desserts altogether, she opted for low-fat puddings, yogurt, fruit, or roasted nuts. While they weren't as gratifying as a warm chocolate-fudge brownie sundae, they eased her cravings. Norma still longed for the super-sweet indulgent desserts, but far less so than during her previous all-or-nothing failed attempts. And she was delighted that she was able to skip dessert occasionally without too much agony.

Norma then made a point of consciously repeating this diet habit for a few weeks. And she asked her best friend to encourage her to forgo desserts whenever they ate out. Eventually, it became a habit—an effortless repeatable behavior. She soon noticed a modest improvement in her weight.

She then decided to go a little further and tackle the rest of her food regimen. She made a deal with a nearby supermarket to deliver food to her house once a week. She focused on ordering a lot of healthful, unprocessed, fresh, and mostly organic foods such as fish, nuts, vegetables, fruits, olive oil, and eggs. She figured that by involving the supermarket in her habit, her chances of going out to buy junk or highly processed foods would significantly decrease. She would also be spared the temptation to pick up unhealthful items while roaming through the aisles on her own.

At the same time, Norma also began to exercise at a gym every other evening after work. But this didn't last long. Understandably, after a long day, it was difficult for her to find the energy to drive for twenty minutes to the gym, then spend an hour there sweating away.

Norma again decided to lower her expectations and adopt a moderate exercise regimen. She contacted a trainer at her gym and made a deal with him to train her twice a week for half an hour. She also informed him that if she didn't show up for a session, she would nonetheless pay him for it. She reasoned that this would give her an incentive not to lose money by missing a session. This was another way to increase her accountability. Also, by bringing a trainer into her new habit, she had someone to support and encourage her.

However, Norma still resented having to drive to the gym after a long day at work. In other words, her brain was still not happy with the deal and would not settle for it. Norma then came to the conclusion that she had to sweeten the deal further in order for her brain to accept it.

She did some thinking and finally hit on the idea of moving the gym to her house! She had a discussion with her trainer, who agreed to train her at her home for a higher fee. That was fine with Norma. She followed through by going online and ordering a variety of weights, a workout bench and two exercise machines, which were all placed in her basement.

The new system worked like a charm. Norma had found truly brilliant solutions to a nagging problem. She had fulfilled the *Three Musketeers* conditions when changing her eating and exercising habits: *she struck a reasonable deal with her brain, she repeated her new habits, and she set up a buddy system to encourage her.*

Ultimately, her newly formed diet and exercise routines were acceptable to her brain. As a result, she was able to stop her unhealthful eating, slim down and regain her self-esteem.

The "Stumbling Sutures" Story

Facelifts are one of the most popular and often-scheduled surgeries I perform.

Soon after I established my clinic, Karen, the fifty-two-year-old wife of a Canadian real estate mogul, came to see me for a facelift. I performed a traditional moderately invasive technique. The recovery was uneventful.

Patrick, her husband, who was in his early sixties, accompanied her to her one-month checkup. He told me he was very pleased with Karen's facelift and was considering one for himself (a not-so-rare occurrence after a spouse's surgery). But there was just one problem: He wasn't ready for the type of facelift his wife had. He was looking for a less invasive procedure, but one that still gave a worthwhile result.

I could have suggested a smaller facelift with a smaller result, but that's not what Patrick was looking for. I had always considered minimally invasive surgery one of my goals, so I was intrigued. I had been presented with an exciting challenge.

A few months later, after extensive reflection and analysis, I came up with an innovative solution. My idea was to pull facial tissues more efficiently—using certain calculations—in order to compensate for the more limited surgery. I started applying this theory to my facelift technique, calling it the "Optimum Mobility facelift." Eventually, I presented it at multiple medical conferences and published an article about it in a leading plastic surgery journal.

This technique had the important advantage of being minimally invasive (limited surgery) as well as effective. But to compensate for the smaller surgery, the technique required the use of specially executed sutures applied to the muscles at predetermined points and at precise angulations, while using a calculated calibrated force.

In other words, this Optimum Mobility facelift, in spite of being less invasive and very patient-friendly, had an unexpected disadvantage for the surgeon: The stitches were technically difficult to perform—hard to adjust and tricky to align in the proper sequence and at the correct rigorous tilt. Therefore, each of the twenty or so stitches took a long time to complete, and often needed to be removed and re-executed if any wasn't satisfactory.

Then I had an idea. I decided to turn each suture application into *a habit*—an automatic routine—by practicing it repeatedly.

To master this, I blocked out one hour every evening and six hours on weekends for a full month. I analyzed the details of the ideal movements and the precise angles required for each stitch. Then, using a foam block, I practiced each stitch in sequence, repeating it hundreds of times. Eventually, I started getting better and faster at it. By the end of the month, I had practiced more than four thousand stitches. And at that point, I was able to complete each stitch easily, with near-perfect precision. What used to be a complicated tactical exercise had become a no-brainer—a habit.

I met Patrick again almost two years after our first conversation and explained my new approach. He opted to have the procedure, and the result was very satisfactory to him, matching his expectations.

So, because I changed a challenging surgical hurdle into a habit, the minimally invasive Optimum Mobility facelift went from a technically complex procedure to a simple one.

And to this day, I can almost perform these tricky sutures with my eyes . . . half closed!

It's Time to Act

Please stop what you're doing—now—and just take two minutes to make a list of just three habits you would like to change.

It could include things as basic as arriving late to work, not calling family and friends as frequently as you should, misplacing your cell phone, or not getting enough sleep. Or it could include more serious behaviors that are bad for your health, such as addiction.

In any case, you need to introduce smart habits to replace the old ones. If a smart habit doesn't last, it means you need to review and implement the *Three Musketeers* conditions and be innovative in doing so.

Eventually, you will succeed in breaking annoying habits, eliminating harmful routines, and completing daunting tasks without having to think about them. You will reach the stage where many of these bad habits simply disappear by themselves.

By then, you would have mastered *the art of automated living!*

RULE 15

in a Pearl Shell

Create Smart Habits That Simplify Your Life
The Magic of Automated Living

- We Are *Creatures of Habit*
- Only an *Effortless Good Habit* Can Overcome an *Effortless Bad One*
  "One Nail In, One Nail Out"
- *To Create Smart Habits, Implement the Three Musketeers Conditions:*
  1 - Offer a Reasonable Deal to Your Brain: Your Brain Will Reject Any Rotten Deal
  2 - Repeat the New Habit for a Month: Repetition Works, Repetition Works
  3 - Get A Buddy System: Another Party Gets into the Habit . . . of Being Part of Your Habit!
- Then, Relax and Enjoy *The Magic of Automated Living*

UNITASK, DON'T MULTITASK

How to Be Laser-Focused and Highly Productive,
Yet Totally Stress-Free and in the Moment

It's a Circus

Sometimes it seems as if everybody's mind is split into two or three.

We want to do it all, at the same time.

We balance one clinging demand on our time after another—viewing a screen, while answering a ring, while talking, while typing, while reading.

Like circus jugglers and acrobats, we throw pins in the air, and spin here, there and everywhere. And our attention is jerked every which way. It's a danger-defying high-wire act. It's both amazing and exhausting.

It's the circus of modern-day life.

You know the drill:

You go for your morning coffee at a café. The lady serving you interrupts an animated conversation with her coworker for the few seconds it takes to listen to your order. Rather than exchanging a pleasantry with you, she focuses her attention elsewhere. As she is preparing your coffee, she immediately resumes her conversation while picking up the phone for a call-in order.

She is multitasking like the best of them.

You arrive at work and stop by a colleague's office to discuss a business matter. He is engrossed in something on his computer, staring at his screen while listening to his office TV play in the background. Without interrupting his computer work, he asks you to explain what you need, all the while continuing his typing and alternating his gaze between you and his computer screen.

Later that day, you arrive home for supper and head straight into the kitchen, eager to tell your spouse about some exciting news at work. Without interrupting her cooking, and while giving instructions to the kids across the room, she says, "Go ahead, dear, I'm listening," without ever looking at you.

Then you sit at the dinner table with your kids, ready to hear about their day at school. But they're staring at their cell phones, texting friends, and playing video games nonstop while they're eating. The family conversation is just background noise.

The Cult of All

It seems that we're living in a new civilization of:

> **Have it all—do it all—all at once!**

From morning until night, our attention spans are like shards of broken glass, splintering our energies in all directions. The result of all that frenzied activity? Poor focus, low efficiency, impaired communications, and sometimes the risk of danger. For example, millions of us drive while listening to music, talking on the phone and checking our text messages, all at once.

And we do the same thing as we drive through our lives. We compulsively multitask, neglecting precious one-on-one time with our family and friends, and overlooking valuable information and cues from our coworkers.

By attempting to have it all and miss nothing, we are actually missing everything.

Lunch: Break or Burden?

It's noon.

Bob is strolling through the park on a warm spring day.

He is relaxed and carefree, immersed in the experience of an outdoor lunch break.

Breathing deeply, he delights in the fragrance of the cherry blossoms and freshly mowed grass. Scanning the winding trails, he observes with interest the parade of joggers, mothers with children, dog walkers, sunbathers, cyclists, in-line skaters, and a group of police officers on horseback.

Just a bit hungry, he impulsively buys himself a warm pretzel from a street vendor and savors the salty crunch and soft center, which he dips in mustard. Munching contentedly, he strolls toward the busking violinist playing Vivaldi on the other side of the park to better enjoy the melody. Appreciating the accomplished performance, he drops a couple of dollars into the old man's basket.

At 12:30 p.m., Bob hears the calendar alarm on his phone, reminding him of his planned ten-minute slot for checking messages. He sits on a bench and focuses on going through his e-mails and texts, answering them briefly as necessary.

As he finishes, he realizes that he still has seven minutes to spare. He came prepared. He opens the book he brought with him, a novel about artificial intelligence, and starts reading. While doing so, he continues to enjoy the violinist, now playing Albinoni. Although absorbed in his fiction, he can still appreciate the music in the background.

His alarm goes off again at 12:55 p.m. He heads back to work, feeling invigorated and refreshed.

Jessica is also spending her lunch break at the same park.

She is tense and distracted, taking shallow breaths as she walks briskly toward a shady spot. Scrunched over a spinach salad (her favorite), she hardly tastes it as she sits on a bench absently talking into her cell phone.

When the call is finished, she continues to angrily reflect on being passed over for a promotion. She doesn't notice the aroma of the pine tree shading her, and she is oblivious to the adorable newborn baby just feet away, smiling up at her from his carriage. Quickly finishing her lunch, she then makes another phone call while screening her social media feeds.

Around 1 p.m., she is back at her desk to resume a stress-filled day, more frazzled than ever.

The moral of these stories?

While Bob was actually in the park, Jessica wasn't!

Bob was reveling in it, while Jessica, like most of us, was just at the park, absent from the moment, preoccupied by her own thoughts and concerns.

How often have we done the same thing? We are *at* the beach with our kids, but we are really a million miles away, multitasking instead of concentrating on the moment. Or we are *at* the Thanksgiving dinner or Christmas tree-trimming party, but we break away to another room to answer a call.

The "Busy for Nothing" Phenomenon

When we multitask, it might seem like we're working fast and efficiently, getting several things done, saving time in the process. That's a myth.

People who think they can partition their attention between a number of things at once aren't actually getting much done. In fact, they are achieving less, performing worse, and getting more stressed out.

In other words:

> **Multitasking means—**
> **being very busy . . . doing very little!**

Here is why.

The "Multiswitching" Phenomenon

According to Canadian author Michael Harris, "When we think we're multitasking, we're actually *multiswitching*." *The brain is simply diverting its attention from one thing to another.*

Physician Amit Sood, author of *The Mayo Clinic Guide to Stress-Free Living*, arrived at the same conclusion: The brain cannot focus consciously on more than one thing at a time.

So, when you're splitting your concentration, your brain is really just toggling between tasks. And each toggle depletes energy. Multitasking drains you and your brain.

Though multitasking is viewed by many as a virtue, it's actually a vice. In fact, research has shown that multitasking can reduce productivity by as much as 40 percent.

In addition, and most important, multitasking interrupts interpersonal communication. Multitasking leads to loneliness, neglected relationships and unappreciated moments in nature.

Therefore, multitasking is a prescription for inefficiency and isolation. We lose our life compass, adrift in the woods of technological overload.

The Smothering Technology

Technology gives us the illusion of connecting and being connected. However, in fact, it's disconnecting us.

Sure, we might get material tasks done simultaneously—typing an e-mail, checking social media, reading news posts, fielding phone messages—but we lose touch with life and with the people and things that are most important to us.

Instead of mastering technology, we have allowed it to master us.

Rather than supporting us, technology is smothering us.

The Here, the Now, and the Somewhere Else

When you're overwhelmed with multiple tasks, you can't focus on the big picture and on what's meaningful in life, namely, connecting with others and savoring the here and now.

In this frenetic culture, it's as if nobody is in the present. We always seem to be somewhere else. We are pulled away by our e-mails, cell phones, television, and work demands, while giving other people only a fraction of our attention. Rather than being fully present for what we're doing in the moment, most of us are cheating that moment by multitasking.

When was the last time you gave 100 percent of your attention to anyone or anything? So often, when you're talking on the phone, you may have multiple browsers open and a few text messages on the go. Or you may be flipping through documents on your desk. All these things are competing for your attention.

The result is the rareness of *the human moment*, such as having dinner with friends, taking a walk, or relaxing on the porch with neighbors. That human moment is distinctly different from *the electronic moment*, which comprises the hours we spend in front of screens.

We must get back to one-on-one connections. We must fully appreciate the presence of other people—savoring our meals together, communicating directly and completely—and truly pay attention to the natural world around us. Nothing equals that.

So, stop multitasking your life.

**Unitask as often as possible
and multitask as seldom as possible.**

By unitasking, you allow yourself to become captivated and consumed by what you're experiencing, whether it's work, a book, a sporting event, or a conversation.

And by addressing one thing at a time, you work efficiently, reduce your stress level, and exponentially increase your enjoyment of life.

The "Follow Your Eyes" Formula

Trying to stop multitasking is like trying to quit smoking. It's an addiction that requires conscious intervention.

The simplest trick is:

Where your eyes go . . . you go!

Let your eyes choose the task.

Here's how this works:

- *When You're Looking at "People," Concentrate Fully*

  When you're having a conversation with someone, look directly at the person speaking, and really listen to what that person has to say.

  Set aside activities and thoughts that could distract you. Don't think about your to-do list. Don't let your mind wander. Don't allow yourself to check your smartphone or computer screen. Instead, give the gift of your undivided attention. *This is your unitask—your only task.*

  Likewise, if you're sitting at the dinner table, be there. Don't rush. Relish the food, savor each bite, and look at the people around the table as you listen to them.

- *When You're Looking at "Things," Concentrate Fully*

At work, focus on what's in front of you. Don't get distracted.

Instead of going back and forth from one job to another, try to fully devote your attention to one task at a time. You will see your efficiency soar and your stress level plummet.

And even when you're alone and looking at whatever you're looking at, like when you're reading, watching TV, exercising, dancing, or gardening, try to appreciate it with all five senses.

The "Follow Your Eyes" formula has one exception—the automated habits. For example, walking on a familiar sidewalk or casually listening to music are passive actions rather than active ones, and may be combined with another task—e.g., walking while talking or working while listening to soft music.

RULE 16

in a Pearl Shell

Unitask,
Don't Multitask
*How to Be Laser-Focused and Highly Productive,
Yet Totally Stress-Free and in the Moment*

- *Don't Be a Circus Acrobat,* Juggling Pins in the Air, Spinning Here, There, and Everywhere
- *Don't Try to Have It All, Do It All, All at Once*
  You Will Be *Very Busy . . .* Doing *Very Little*
- *Unitask* as Often as Possible, *Multitask* as Seldom as Possible
- And Let Your *Eyes* Choose the Unitask:
  Where Your Eyes Go . . . You Go!

FLIP THE FREEBIE ...
AND LOOK FOR
THE HIDDEN PRICE TAG!

Nothing Is Free

The "Something for Nothing" Phenomenon

In business and in life, every action creates an *impact*.

> **Everything that happens between people is ... an exchange.**

As stated in Newton's third law of motion: *"For every action, there is an equal and opposite reaction."*

This law of nature isn't only pertinent to physics; it also applies to everything else in our lives. And its conclusion is just as true today as it was when Newton stated it back in 1687:

A something gives an equal something in return, and
a nothing gives an equal nothing in return.

This applies to any sort of exchange between people.

> **You can get something—in return**
> **for something,**
> *but you can't get something—*
> *for nothing!*

In other words:

> **Whenever you receive anything for free ... be suspicious!**

For example, people and businesses will offer you things that have hidden conditions attached to them. Whenever you receive an unbelievably good offer, a gift or an unexpected invitation, make sure there are no strings attached and no hidden obligations on your part. Even an unexpected call or a bit of exaggerated flattery should raise a red flag.

Ask yourself, *What's the motive behind this generous offer or compliment?*

> The bigger the too-good-to-be-true offer—
> the higher the risk—
> and the more skeptical you should be.

So, when a marketing company, a long-lost friend, or a cold business call presents an opportunity, do the same thing you would do when you receive a birthday gift and wonder about its real cost:

> Flip it over . . . to look for *the hidden price tag!*

Ask yourself what the giver is planning to get from you in return—which is often of equal or greater value than the freebie. *Whoever is giving you something out of the blue will likely expect to get back something of similar or greater value.*

Even when people give freely, seemingly compassionately, there is nearly always a payoff for the giver. For example, when a new neighbor pays you a visit, he or she is expecting you to be friendly in return; when you make a large donation to a charity, unless you give anonymously, you await the satisfaction that comes from public recognition; and when you give a friend a Christmas gift, you expect him or her to reciprocate with a gift of similar value. There is always an underlying reward of some kind. It's Newton's law again!

And it's the same in business. For example, when you're shopping at a mall, you're constantly being pitched. As you stroll by stores, you may be offered a complimentary piece of chocolate (to entice you to buy a whole box) or a sample vial of perfume (again, to encourage you to buy a whole bottle). The same goes for a free makeup application or a barbecue demonstration. These freebies are designed to seduce or intimidate you into buying something of greater value. You always have to be on the alert for ways in which you may be subtly manipulated into providing the reciprocity that other people expect from you.

Newton's third law even applies to situations that seem selfless on the surface. For example, what could be more altruistic than a mother caring for her newborn baby? Certainly, what a mother does for an infant is a one-sided donation of love and care, right? Wrong. The mother is getting back something at least as valuable as her apparent sacrifice—the joy of seeing her baby content, which in turn brings her happiness and satisfaction.

When we truly love another human being, we definitely get an emotional payoff. In such a case, the gift of love is compensated by an inner remuneration, an emotional reward of at least equal value. Likewise, when religious individuals give anonymously, without seeking recognition, they still derive a spiritual contentment from being virtuous.

So, for every action, there is an equal and opposite reaction—always.

Never accept a freebie without wondering about what's expected of you, because:

**For almost every freebie—sooner or later—
something of an equal or higher value will be either:
Taken away from you ... or given away by you.**

Almost always!

Blows Worth Billions

Here is a true story about a swindler who had his victims convinced that he could give them *something for nothing*.

Disgraced financier Bernie Madoff was convicted in 2009 for operating the biggest investment scam in history. His Ponzi scheme defrauded 4,800 clients of almost $65 billion. Before he was caught, his net worth was estimated at $17 billion, much of it stolen.

How did Madoff succeed in such epic proportions? He had what it took: a criminal mind, a talent for stealth, brazen self-confidence, a megalomaniacal lust for money, and an ability to talk anyone into anything.

Affable and very charismatic, he was loved by family and friends, adored by employees, and highly admired by colleagues. He impressed potential clients with an extraordinary show of wealth: private jets, a Manhattan penthouse, and a yacht docked on the French Riviera, all of which he acquired by spending his investors' money!

Armed with a convincing blueprint for success, Madoff projected himself as a top-notch business genius. He was one of Wall Street's preeminent power brokers, a star in the world of white-collar finance who even managed to hold a Nasdaq chairmanship.

Madoff tricked experienced private investors and established organizations alike, dangling awesome investment opportunities in front of them and promising unparalleled high returns. He reassured them with bogus monthly statements that showed the value of their investments going through the roof.

When some of them started to raise doubts and request their money back, Madoff refunded them immediately, along with their promised unbelievable returns. This convinced the investors that: *It's too good to be true, but it's true!* And they came back with more money.

These affluent investors believed they could defy common sense and fool the market, but they ended up fooling themselves. Eager to quickly make a fortune, they were readily seduced and fell victim to Madoff's grand hoax. Their greed was the perfect foil for his own ambition.

They ignored at their peril an old adage:

When it sounds *too good to be true* ... it is!

Although Madoff was sentenced to 150 years in prison (in 2021, he died in prison at the age of 82), his punishment was small comfort to his thousands of victims. They all naively attempted to get something for nothing, and ended up in financial ruin, their fortunes gone.

When I Was Hit Hard by an Austrian Ball!

As long-time residents of Montreal, Stephanie and I regularly attend *Le Bal Viennois de Montréal,* the city's annual Austrian ball, a fairy-tale evening where attendees dance the night away in gowns, and white tie and tails.

The event blends European traditions with modern luxuries for the benefit of a charitable cause. It takes place at Le Château Champlain, an elegant hotel equipped with a beautiful ballroom and a gigantic dance floor. Stephanie, who is of Austrian heritage, relishes the cultural atmosphere, while I love practicing ballroom dancing.

On one such night, we were seated next to a Turkish businessman, Mr. Ozturk, and his wife, an affable couple in their forties. During the course of our conversation, I mentioned that we were planning a family vacation to Antalya, a Turkish resort city on the southern Mediterranean. Mr. Ozturk insisted on meeting us upon our arrival.

Six months later, as we landed in Istanbul, there was Mr. Ozturk's driver waiting for us at the airport. He drove us to the Ciragan Palace Kempinski, a luxury hotel with the feeling of a genuine Ottoman Empire palace. Stephanie and I and our two children, Amanda and Michael, were escorted to a beautiful suite and informed by the hotel that our two-night stay was courtesy of Mr. Ozturk. We were overwhelmed by his generosity.

That same evening, Mr. Ozturk and his family took us out for a lavish dinner. It was a great evening: Mr. Ozturk's son and daughter were around the same ages as our children, which helped cement the bonds between our families.

During our stay at the Antalya beach resort, the Ozturk family came to join us for three days. And as always, Mr. Ozturk continued to be the gracious host. His hospitality was touching.

Near the end of our stay, Mr. Ozturk casually disclosed to me that he was thinking of opening a plastic surgery clinic in Istanbul, a facility where I could perform surgery on a regular basis. He was convinced the enterprise would be lucrative, especially because his circle of wealthy friends and associates favored foreign surgeons. He offered to furnish 75 percent of the initial investment if I contributed the remaining 25 percent share.

It sounded like a promising opportunity—a viable business plan that could give my practice an international presence. By the end of the vacation, I was convinced that Mr. Ozturk's project had a high chance for success, and I felt that I could trust him.

I was mesmerized by his freebies. And I never questioned them, nor did I look for the hidden price tag. Too bad I hadn't yet discovered this rule then!

Once I returned to Canada, I wired an impressive sum of money to Mr. Ozturk's Istanbul bank account, as I had promised I would. Mr. Ozturk traveled to Montreal three months later for a business trip, and he assured me that everything was in motion for the clinic's opening. He said he was busily searching for the ideal space and medical support staff. He promised that, upon his return home, I could expect a call within the month with all the details.

That call never came. And Mr. Ozturk disappeared from the face of the earth.

Whether he was genuine in his attempt to open a clinic but misspent the money, or whether he planned to scam me from the outset, I will never know.

What I know for sure is that my money was gone. And that all those freebies were very costly indeed!

RULE 17

in a Pearl Shell

Flip the Freebie...
and Look for the Hidden Price Tag!
Nothing Is Free

- *For Every Freebie,* Something of an *Equal or Higher Value* Will Be Either:
  Taken Away from You ... or *Given Away* by You!
  Almost Always!
- *When It Sounds Too Good to Be True ... It Is!*

PEOPLE DON'T CHANGE

And Even If They Do Change,
They Often Change Back!

A Cluster of Kids

Glance into a typical first-grade classroom and observe all the six-year-olds interacting with one another and with their teacher.

See that some of them are shy, thoughtful, and compliant, while others are loud, assertive, argumentative, and chattering away confidently. Notice that some are kind and respectful while others are impertinent and antagonistic. See that some are naturally happy and smiling while others are serious and moody. And observe that still others are alert, fast learners, organized, and studious, while others are distracted and unmotivated.

Take note of all these differences because what you see are personality traits that are unlikely to change. In fact, what you see is a reliable prognosis for the future. It's likely to endure even thirty years from now, regardless of future life circumstances, careers, or relationships.

According to psychologist Erik Erikson, personalities stay pretty much the same from early childhood right through our senior years. So, this assortment of children's personalities and talents won't probably turn out any different in adulthood.

The main traits will remain, no matter what!

Nature or Nurture?

Do children inherit the personality traits of their parents? Or are their personalities shaped by their upbringing?

In other words, are personalities and talents the result of our genes or our environment?

Putting it differently: is it biology or social conditioning?

Far Apart, Yet Close as Could Be

Researchers at the University of Minnesota conducted a twenty-year study of 350 pairs of twins, some of whom were reared far apart, in separate households, under contrasting socioeconomic circumstances, and by parents of widely diverse personalities.

Guess what they found? They discovered that the personalities and talents of the sets of twins were very similar, even when the children were raised in different families.

Other studies have revealed that adopted children show traits that are more similar to those of their biological parents than those of their adoptive parents.

Conclusion? The genetic makeup of children has more influence on their personalities and talents than child rearing.

> **Biology wins over environment.**

Our personalities and talents are encrypted into our genes. No wonder people are hard to change!

Here is a solid law of nature:

> **People don't change easily.**
> **And even if they do change . . . they often tend to revert back.**

So, don't waste too much of your time and hopes trying to change people you know, such as family members, friends, or colleagues.

For example, don't view someone you're dating as a potential fixer-upper. If you think you will be able to change that individual's personality and make him or her more romantic, more ambitious, or more anything, forget it.

Sara's Story

Sarah, one of Stephanie's friends, craved financial security, but she tended to choose her romantic partners based on their good looks rather than their careers or personalities. Physical chemistry was her temptation, monetary security, her need.

When she met Don, a handsome personal trainer, she was convinced that he had a promising future. He assured her that he was going to open a gym of his own, create a franchise, and establish a solid financial future for both of them.

It never happened. Don was Mr. Promise. He was well-meaning but not blessed with business acumen. He was all talk and no action. Worse, he was also careless and a big spender.

Convinced that she could change him, Sarah confronted him on multiple occasions. She attempted, time and again, using her standard repertoire of arguments, pleas, and threats, to keep him on track. Don would get serious and disciplined for a month or two, and Sarah would be ecstatic. But invariably he would relapse.

He couldn't meet her need for financial security, and she couldn't accept and enjoy him as he was.

Ultimately, they broke up.

Stop Squeezing

As we know deep down, from our dealings with family members, friends, colleagues, or acquaintances: *People don't change easily unless they want to do so on their own.*

This inability to change applies to personality traits (attitudes, character, temperament), as well as talents (aptitudes, skills, abilities).

You may be tempted to think, *If only they would be more considerate, more loyal, more caring, more punctual, more prudent, wiser with money, or more hard-working.*

Nope. Not going to happen.

So:

> **Try once or twice to change someone ... then give it up.**

Beyond that, trying to change that person is like trying to get water out of a stone. No matter how hard you squeeze the stone, chances are you won't get a single drop of water!

Therefore, when you aren't obtaining what you need from people after asking twice, then stop asking.

> **Stop making the *same request*—to the *same people*.**

Quit squeezing the stone!

Now comes the big question:

If people won't change, what can you do to get what you want?

Some studies have shown that, although unlikely to significantly change, *personalities may sometimes be slightly modified over time, in a subtle way.*

So, is there another approach that may work to accomplish your goal without squeezing any stones?

Yes, there is. It's the next universal rule!

RULE 18

in a Pearl Shell

People Don't Change
And Even If They Do Change, They Often Change Back!

- *Biology Wins Over Environment*
  Personalities Are Encrypted into Our Genes
- *People Don't Change Easily*
  And Even If They *Do Change*, They Tend to *Revert Back*
- *Try Just Once or Twice to Change Them*
  Then, *Quit Squeezing the Stone*, and Follow Rule 19!

SEED A
WILL GIVE YOU
PLANT A . . .
EVERY SINGLE TIME

If You Want a Different Plant,
Try a Different Seed!

The "Mango Vines" Story

Leslie, a Florida homemaker, loves mangoes so much that she decides to grow a mango tree in her backyard. She does some research online, then orders the best mango seeds she can find.

When the package arrives, she is so excited that she doesn't even look at it. She just rips it open. She can't wait to get into her backyard and start digging. She has the perfect spot all picked out.

After planting the seeds, she carries out her botanical project with great enthusiasm for the next few weeks. She diligently waters the soil, eagerly awaiting the beautiful tree that will eventually produce delicious mangoes.

But alas, when the plant emerges from the ground, it's an impostor—it isn't a mango tree, it's a tomato vine!

How could this have happened? Distraught, Leslie runs to her kitchen drawer and checks the label on the seed package. It clearly reads: sweet vine tomatoes.

She then wonders what to do. She could return the seed package for a refund, but this would take too long. Plus, she feels she isn't in the mood to wait for another order.

Instead, she hopes for the best and decides to try again—with the same seeds! Perhaps the package was mislabeled, she reasons.

A few weeks later, she gets another tomato vine!

Does she give up and accept the obvious? No way. Undeterred, Leslie gives it a third try. The result: yet another tomato vine, and no mango tree in sight!

Haven't we all been guilty, at times, of Leslie's amazing irrational insistence on getting a different outcome from repeating the same procedure?

It's time to learn some lessons from Leslie's story

Leslie's Lesson I

Don't Expect Miracles in Agriculture: Seed A Yields Plant A

The first lesson of Leslie's story is evident: You harvest what you sow, and nothing will change that.

If you sow seed A, it will grow into plant A . . . every single time, no matter how desperate you are for plant B.

Leslie's Lesson II
Don't Expect Miracles in Life Either: Action A Gives Reaction A
If you take action A with someone, it will elicit reaction A from that person . . . every single time. This will happen no matter how desperate you are to achieve reaction B instead.

Yet, in life:

> We often repeat the same thing . . . and expect a different outcome!

We bang our heads against the wall, expecting a different, more satisfactory response. And we become frustrated when it doesn't happen.

Leslie's Lesson III
Repetition Doesn't Work: Einstein's Theory of Insanity
Albert Einstein could well have been thinking of Leslie and her mangoes (excuse me—tomatoes), when he apparently said, "The definition of insanity is doing the same thing over and over again and expecting different results."

In other words, if we try something once or twice and it fails, we will get the same result the third, fourth and fifth times as well.

Consider the case of Julie, a good-hearted daughter.

Her mother is a mostly ungrateful sourpuss. Julie repeatedly does favors for her, but her mother always finds fault with each of them. She'll say things such as, "Why did you buy me red apples instead of green ones?" or "I returned the perfume because I couldn't walk around smelling like that." Julie then gets upset, her mother apologizes, and Julie resumes her doomed attempts to please her.

She is constantly planting flowers, and constantly reaping weeds.

Leslie's Lesson IV
If People Can't Change, You Create the Change:
The Ball Is in Your Court

You need to focus on getting what you want from people—i.e., what's good for you, which, in many cases, is also good for them.

You may achieve this, not by trying to change them, but by you changing your approach to them.

In other words:

> The change should come from YOU.

When you fail to achieve the desired response, don't try the same action repeatedly.

> If you want a different reaction from people . . .
> try a different action.

Because:

> By changing your *action* . . .
> you change people's *reaction*.

Julie tried this approach the following Mother's Day. After giving her mom a beautiful blue cotton sweater, the mom predictably responded, "Julie, you should know I only wear wool, and this isn't my color."

"No problem, Mom," Julie responded calmly. "I understand that your tastes differ from mine. Here is the receipt. Just return the sweater and get what you like." Julie's mother was speechless. She ended up returning the sweater and never again spoke crossly to her daughter.

The lesson of the story? Julie didn't try to persuade her mother to change. She, herself, initiated a change in her own behavior. She planted a new seed and obtained a new result.

You can apply this approach in so many everyday situations.

For example:

You have warned your office cleaner about his sloppy work (action A), but nothing has changed (reaction A). The next time, you create the change by trying something different: You tell the cleaner that you will only pay 75 percent of his fee until his cleaning improves (action B). He does make an effort at first, but falls into his old patterns within a few weeks (reaction B). Finally, *you* initiate another change by hiring a new cleaning person (action C). Your office is now spotless (reaction C). Perfect.

Here is another scenario:

Your spouse is always late for appointments. It's exasperating and the source of many arguments. Over the years, you have tried to persuade him or her to be on time (action A), but your pleas have always fallen on deaf ears (reaction A). The next time, *you* create the change by trying something different. You tell your spouse that dinner is at 7 p.m. when it's really at 8 p.m. (action B). You end up leaving the house at eight. This is a definite improvement, but still not good enough (reaction B). On the following occasion, you tell your spouse that the reservation is at 6:30 p.m. when it's really at 8 p.m. (action C). Congrats! You both leave on time and arrive on time (reaction C).

A final example:

You know an attractive colleague at work whom you would really like to date, but she seems unapproachable. She is always been pleasant and polite but distant. You tried once to ask her for a date (action A), but she politely refused (reaction A). The second time, *you* create the change by trying something different: you send her a bouquet of flowers (action B). She texts you a thank-you note, but she still wouldn't go out with you (reaction B). Then you learn from a mutual friend that she is a basketball fan. You buy two tickets for an NBA game and arrange to deliver one as a gift to her home (action C). She agrees to attend the game with you, sits next to you for two and a half hours, and accepts a late dinner invitation following the game (reaction C).

The bottom line:
You have to be innovative and find the right action that will get you what you want.

A Roman-Inspired Violinist

During one of our summer family vacations in Rome, Stephanie, Amanda, Michael and I went out for dinner. Our hotel concierge recommended a pleasant restaurant for us, Ai Tre Tartufi, located on the picturesque Piazza Navona.

From our table, we enjoyed a view of the delightful Quattro Fiumi fountain. Adding to the atmosphere was a young violinist serenading everyone within earshot. His performance was exquisite.

Michael, who was fifteen at the time, had been taking violin lessons for three years. He rose from the table and spent almost an hour listening to and watching the Italian virtuoso. When he returned to our table for his meal, he seemed pensive.

As we were served dessert, he looked at me intently.

"How would you feel about me becoming a violinist?" he asked.

I smiled and answered, "You *are* a violinist."

However, that wasn't what Michael meant. "I want to be a *real* violinist," he said. "After I get my high school diploma, I don't want to go to college. Instead, I would like to go to a conservatory so I can play violin for a living."

At first, I thought he was joking. Michael was a straight A student, highly regarded by his teachers. Skipping college wasn't exactly what I had envisioned for him. Stephanie and Amanda tried to convince him that he should at least get a university degree to secure his future before deciding on what to do with his musical abilities. They reminded him that he was doing especially well in school and that he would likely be able to apply to any university he chose.

Michael held firm, insisting on his new aspiration. For the time being, though, I decided not to argue with him. I figured that by the time we arrived back in Montreal, he would have forgotten all about this fanciful ambition.

He didn't. When he resumed school, I noticed that Michael was practicing the violin daily for hours at a time, which meant he wasn't studying as much as he had previously. By late September, his first monthly report card was conclusive: he had gone from straight As to Bs in many subjects.

This precipitous drop in his academic performance worried me. I wasn't sure what to do. I had failed once to get him to change his mind by just letting him be. My seed A had given me a good-for-nothing plant A.

I also saw that Stephanie's and Amanda's reasoning with him had gone nowhere. Repeating their argument with him would have been futile—even insane, according to Einstein. I had to figure out a new seed to plant, a new action. The change had to come from *me*.

I initially thought about taking away Michael's violin or canceling his lessons until he did better in school. By doing so, I would have obviously forced him to work harder, but he would have never been as eager to study and excel as he had been. I knew from being a teacher myself that *eagerness is the secret potion of achievers*. So, I set aside this plan and came up with another idea.

For action B, I sat with Michael and told him that I didn't mind his becoming a violinist as long as he would be one of the best in the field. He said he would be! But I insisted on hearing his teacher's verdict on that matter and called her myself.

The teacher told me that although Michael was a deft player, she couldn't be certain at that point whether he could develop into a truly distinguished instrumentalist. She added that Michael needed more lessons in order for him, and her, to discern his future potential. This made him even more obsessed with his dream.

I had to create another change—action C. I offered Michael two violin lessons per week rather than one, but on the condition that his marks went back to straight As. I also promised him that I would respect his choice of career. Michael, knowing me, knew that I meant it, and that my word was my bond.

Michael did so well in school from that point forward that he ended up receiving *The Canadian Governor General's Academic Medal*, given to the Canadian student who achieves the highest average upon graduating from high school.

By that time, he had also come to realize that, although he was a competent musician, he could never hope to match the accomplished tonality of Yehudi Menuhin or the melodic grace of Stéphane Grappelli. He therefore decided to apply most of his efforts to the field of engineering.

Eventually he obtained his degree and completed a master's and a PhD in biomedical engineering.

And yes, he still loves to play violin—as a hobby!

My resolved dilemma with Michael is a perfect example of how you can get what's good for you or for the people you care about most, not by them changing their attitude, but by you changing yours. The change comes from you.

The ball is in your court!

RULE 19

in a Pearl Shell

Seed A
Will Give You
Plant A...
Every Single Time
If You Want a Different Plant, Try a Different Seed!

- Remember Einstein's Theory of Insanity:
  Repetition Doesn't Work
- Don't Do the *Same Thing* Over and Over Again, While
  Expecting a *Different Result*
- If You Plant *Seed A*, It Will Grow into *Plant A...*
  Every Single Time
- And If You Take *Action A*, It Will Elicit *Reaction A...*
  Every Single Time
- *The Change Has to Come from YOU*
  By Changing Your Action, You Change People's Reaction
- *The Ball Is in Your Court!*

THINK OF WHAT YOU HAVE,

NOT WHAT YOU DON'T HAVE

And Think of What Other People
DON'T Have,
Not What They DO Have

The "Relativity" Phenomenon

Human beings can't resist comparing themselves to other human beings, regardless of race, nationality, political affiliation or economic status.

How often do we compare ourselves to other people? We're always wondering how we measure up to others in the game of life, and where we are relative to where they are. We observe their lives from the outside, admiring their material possessions, presumed bank accounts, vacations, career advancements, good health or good looks, and contrast our fortunes to theirs.

It's a cycle of relativity. *It's compare and despair!*

The result? Jealousy fosters discontent and distress. And the more we compare, the less happy we feel and the more we want.

The "In Sight—Therefore—In Mind" Phenomenon

Like all of us, you tend to compare yourself to the people within your world bubble. These may include immediate and extended family members, friends, colleagues at work, neighbors, or other people within your social circles.

For example:

Your brother-in-law was just given a huge promotion, you weren't;

Your friend is in a happy marriage, you're still having trouble dating;

Your coworkers are getting all the best client accounts, you're not;

Your college acquaintance has five thousand Facebook followers; you have a few hundred;

The guy at the gym has a six-pack and a full head of hair, you're rather stout with a receding hairline;

Your brother just built a huge home, you're struggling to pay the rent.

And on and on it goes.

It's a universal truth that comparing ourselves to people in our proximity seems to be part of our DNA.

Even in situations that have nothing to do with competition, the compare addiction is affected by the "In Sight—Therefore—In Mind" phenomenon.

The "Out of Sight—Therefore—Out of Mind" Phenomenon

On the other hand, people who live outside our *bubble* aren't likely to incite our envy. They are beyond the range of our Jealousy-O-Meter!

They're out of sight, therefore, out of mind.

We may feel envious of a colleague's promotion or lavish vacation, but we are not bothered in the least by the billionaires we see on the news traveling on private jets and yachts. And if a close friend has cancer, we instantly worry about our own health far more than we ordinarily would if we had watched a documentary about the millions of cancer patients worldwide.

It doesn't hit as hard when it's far from home.

The Game-Changer List

When you compare yourself to others, you forget what you're blessed with, and only remember what you're missing.

So, since you can't change this hereditary comparison obsession, can you at least change the rules of the compare-and-despair game?

Here is a way to beat this comparison malady:

> **Make your gratitude list—today.**

Do It Now, Perfect It Later (Rule 1). This list will shift your focus to the goodness in life, to the things you do have. And it will erase your sense of ingratitude for the things you don't have. You will be amazed at how long your list will turn out to be—surprised at how many blessings you always took for granted.

For example, you may have all or most of the following: fresh air to breathe; good food to eat; a warm bed to sleep in; family and friends; healthy children; and the ability to walk, talk, hear, see, and smell.

Now sit back, take a look at your gratitude list, and be thankful. Don't repeat the mistake of author Agatha Christie, who realized, too late, that, "One doesn't recognize the really important moments in one's life until it's too late."

If you don't appreciate what you have now, you may realize, *too late* as well, how lucky you were, and regret every single minute you spent worrying about what you don't have.

Remember what you *have*—not what you *don't have*.

If you do, you will win two precious gifts in one fell swoop: wisdom and, most important, contentment.

Cravings Never Quenched

"He is not poor that hath not much, but he that craves much," the seventeenth-century historian Thomas Fuller rightly stated.

Comparing yourself to others and craving what you don't have is harmful if you do it unwisely: "Why don't I have this?" and "Why should they have that?"

However, comparing yourself to others can be beneficial if you do it smartly: "Thank God I have this" and "Isn't it unfortunate that they don't have what I have?"

Practice this grateful type of comparison, and you will gain inner peace forever.

Count your blessings—not your sorrows.

Instead of grumbling about your shortcomings, be grateful for your assets.

And remember that whatever you possess in life, whether it's money, status, looks, or health, there will always be someone, somewhere, who will beat you at it.

Your cravings will never be quenched!

The Grass Is Not Greener

We tend to believe that the grass is greener on the other side.

> We only see what other people are blessed with—
> rather than what they're missing.

But chances are that we'll never find out what those other people are missing. This is because, like all of us, they only project a blissful picture of their lives. People broadcast their good news, but hide their not-so-flattering sides, whether social, marital, professional, wealth-related, or anything else.

So, if we keep comparing our fortunes to those of others, we should at least consider what they may be missing, which we may actually have.

For example, how many of us have admired the extraordinary accomplishments and wealth of Steve Jobs? He certainly seemed to have it all and was the envy of millions of people.

But we only looked at what he had, not what he didn't have—until the news of his terminal disease was disclosed. All his money meant little as he faced pancreatic cancer, ultimately losing that battle at age fifty-six. That's young.

How many older people are blessed with years of life beyond that, yet all they do is complain?!

The "What Could Have Happened" Question

The next time you're feeling disappointed about your souring relationships or failing fortunes, ask yourself one simple question:

> **What are the misfortunes that**
> *could have happened to me ... but didn't?*

When you remember the numerous times you escaped disaster, you will feel blessed.

For example, when you had that growth on your back removed, it might have been cancerous, but it wasn't; or when you had that accident on the highway, you could have been killed or gravely injured, but you weren't; or when your baby was born after an emergency C-section, any number of physical problems could have occurred, but didn't. You wound up with a healthy baby.

All you have to do is watch the evening news or pick up a newspaper to see how fortunate you are. There are heartbreaking calamities everywhere you look—mishaps, death, disease, epidemics, and deprivation of every kind. Thankfully, you have been spared most of them. In fact, in your daily life, things go just fine most of the time.

Be grateful and celebrate.

RULE 20

in a Pearl Shell

Think of What You Have, Not What You Don't Have

And Think of What Other People DON'T Have, Not What They DO Have

- *Stop Comparing and Despairing*
  Count Your Blessings, Not Your Sorrows
- Remember What You *Have*, Not What You *Don't Have*
- Don't Complain About What You're Missing, Because:
  You Will Never Find Out ... What the Others Are Missing
  People Air Their Good News, But Hide Their Not-So-
  Flattering Sides
- *Your Cravings Will Never Be Quenched*
  Whatever You Achieve in Life, There Will Always Be
  Someone Else Who Will Beat You at It!
- Make Your *Gratitude List,* Today
- *Remember the Misfortunes That Could Have Happened to*
  You ... But Didn't
  Then, Be Grateful and Celebrate

LEARNING FROM YOUR OWN MISTAKES IS GOOD,

LEARNING FROM OTHER PEOPLE'S MISTAKES IS EVEN BETTER!

*It's Smarter to Use
a Scientifically Tested Medicine,
Than to Try an Experimental One*

THE MARTIAL ART OF LEARNING FROM YOUR OWN MISTAKES

When YOU Pay the Price

Making mistakes in life is inevitable.

At every stage of development, from childhood to old age, we all stumble in one way or another. As human beings, our judgment isn't always perfect.

You have heard the expression, "I could kick myself." When you make a mistake, it's regrettable. But then there is the emotional aftermath: that combination of guilt, remorse, shame and self-recrimination. It's a torturous feeling that can keep us wide awake at night.

Mistakes typically cause us, and other people, pain and aggravation.

However, there is an assumption that young people should be encouraged to take chances in life, to be free to make mistakes and learn from them. That's somewhat true. When kids try and fail, they learn the art of overcoming initial defeat. They learn to develop their social skills and build up their resilience. Mistakes help children realize what's right and wrong, which is essential to raising confident, capable, happy, and successful adults. And hopefully, as adults, they won't repeat those same mistakes.

The bottom line is:

> Doing the right thing to start with is always best.
> But making mistakes can have a beneficial outcome—
> *only if we learn something from them.*

Brazilian Torture

Eric, a twenty-five-year-old schoolteacher, walked happily into the Los Angeles Combat Sport Club floating in his *gi*, the traditional white garment used for martial arts practice. He was about to have his first private lesson in Brazilian Jiu-Jitsu, a martial art based on grappling and ground fighting.

His instructor, Renzo, had a squarish, muscular body and a fearsome face that bore a constant frown. He was known to be tough and demanding on his students, but he had trained some of the best in the sport.

When Renzo first met Eric, he informed him, in a no-nonsense tone, that he would demonstrate on Eric some Jiu-Jitsu techniques, one after another—without any prior explanation. It was up to Eric to figure out, on his own, how to block each aggressive move.

In other words, Eric had to learn from his own mistakes.

As Renzo applied his first move, the startled Eric found himself punched, clobbered, grabbed, and abruptly thrown off balance across the floor mat. Renzo then repeated the maneuver several times, while the defenseless helpless Eric tried desperately to figure out how to block it. Finally, when the overwhelmed Eric caught on and began to defend himself, Renzo congratulated him with a single word: "Good!"

Renzo immediately applied his second move, and Eric found himself once again hammered, kicked, punched, and then flipped upside down and nearly strangled. After enduring three agonizing acrobatic stunts, the shattered Eric finally managed to evade this second maneuver, but now he felt disoriented, was seeing double, and was limping with a swollen ankle.

Eric was thanking God for surviving this near-annihilation! He was learning from his own mistakes and slowly gaining experience, but at an agonizing price. And he thought that what he went through up to that point was plenty of experience indeed for a first lesson!

At that moment, the desperate Eric, summoning his courage, decided to let Renzo know, in no uncertain terms, that it was time to end his first Jiu-Jitsu lesson.

But before he could utter a single word, he found himself propelled upside down once again, then hurled in every possible direction, shoved, twisted like a pretzel, then slammed onto the floor by what's called a "scissor takedown."

And by the time Eric figured out how to block this third technique, he couldn't even remember his own name!

The moral of the story?

> **Learning from your own mistakes,**
> **though rewarding, can be—painful indeed.**

THE FINE ART OF LEARNING FROM OTHER PEOPLE'S MISTAKES

When THEY Pay the Price

Learning from your mistakes can be a worthwhile experience.

However, there is an even smarter idea:

> **Instead of just learning from your own mistakes—**
> **learn as well from other people's mistakes!**

As a young man, I read numerous philosophy and self-help books. I perused historical novels and autobiographies, and studied what caused protagonists to fail or falter and how they overcame their challenges. I was also on the lookout for practical guidance from other sources. I regularly sought advice from anyone, in any field, with any experience.

And I took reams of notes about these pearls of wisdom. "Learn from the mistakes of others. You can't live long enough to make them all yourself," Eleanor Roosevelt once said.

I love that.

Triple Trips to Heaven

To Catherine, this particular morning was like no other.

A twenty-two-year-old soprano, she was a student at L'Académie de L'Opéra de Paris. Already starting to get noticed in her native Belgium, she had gone to Paris to fine-tune her vocal technique and earn a diploma from that prestigious institution.

What was extraordinary about this morning was that Catherine had been chosen by the academy to meet with world-renowned British soprano Helena Moore of the Royal Opera House, in London's Covent Garden. Ms. Moore was in Paris for three weeks to perform in Mozart's *Die Zauberflöte*, and she graciously offered to tutor one of the academy's students. Catherine, who was the top vocal talent in her class, was chosen.

The 2 p.m. meeting was to take place at L'Opéra National de Paris. Catherine had been up since 5 a.m. because she was just too excited to sleep. By 1 p.m., there she was in front of the big steps of Le Palais Garnier, home of the Opéra, an hour early, dressed in her favorite bright blue suit and wearing high heels to match the formality of the occasion.

Arriving five minutes late in a stretch white limousine, Ms. Moore was welcomed by the opera director, who introduced Catherine to her. The three of them then went through the colossal doors.

As Catherine walked up Le Grand Escalier, the majestic white marble Grand Staircase, she was flabbergasted by the towering pedestals on either side, topped with torchères holding magnificent golden candlesticks.

Then the opera director escorted them through Le Grand Foyer, with its ornate architectural details, intricately painted mosaic-covered domed ceiling, and dazzling gigantic crystal chandeliers.

Catherine was enchanted. This was beyond a dream.

She was in heaven!

When the group finally reached the famous stage, a pianist was eagerly awaiting the acclaimed guest. Catherine felt as if she were reliving scenes from *The Phantom of the Opera*, the musical based on Gaston Leroux's 1910 novel, which is set in this magnificent building. Catherine was then expecting Ms. Moore to choose an aria for her to sing, then give her some recommendations for improving her performance. But instead, Ms. Moore looked at her and said, "Catherine, my dear, you can choose to sing any aria from any opera, and I will give you some tips on it afterward."

Taken aback, Catherine hesitated for a moment, then mustered her courage and answered, "I will try to sing Bellini's aria 'Casta Diva' from *Norma*."

Ms. Moore chuckled and said, "You've got guts, Catherine. You have chosen the hardest aria for a soprano to perform. I haven't sung it myself for years. But I'll tell you what: I will try singing it first, then I will be in a better position to guide you through it."

Accompanied by the pianist, Ms. Moore began singing, occasionally interrupting herself to adjust her tone or timing. During it all, Catherine was listening intently—*and learning*.

And she was so thrilled, and in heaven again!

Twenty minutes later, Ms. Moore was satisfied with her own performance, which Catherine thought was truly regal. It was almost 3 p.m.

A true Brit, Ms. Moore had requested to have high tea served. There, onto the stage, came two waiters in black tie bearing elegant Royal Doulton china, Earl Grey tea, and a few delicious raisin scones with jam and clotted cream.

Catherine was in heaven for the third time!

When her turn came to sing, Catherine, armed with the fresh memory of watching, listening to, and learning from Ms. Moore, performed better than she expected. She even heard a "*Brava*" from the diva, in addition to some pertinent advice.

The whole afternoon was an unforgettable adventure for Catherine, from the extravagant opera house, to the lavish high tea service, to the exuberant experience with Ms. Moore.

However, what Catherine liked most was watching the star soprano making mistakes and self-correcting them, while she, Catherine, took mental notes. Then, when it was her turn to try this most challenging aria, Catherine had already learned how to improve her rendition of it from watching and listening to how the diva had sung it.

The moral of the story?

> Learning from other people's mistakes
> is rewarding—and painless.

THE DILIGENT ART OF
REMEMBERING MISTAKES

Bad Memory Is Bad for You

Most people either make their own mistakes or learn by watching other people make them. They then vow not to repeat those mistakes.

The problem, however, is that lasting impressions are far from guaranteed.

Our memory for self-improvement is short-lived. We forget our learned lessons easily. And we tend to relapse sooner or later.

But is there any way to remember mistakes we have done or seen others do?

Yes, there is.

One Sentence, on Paper

How can you program yourself to remember mistakes, and avoid repeating them?

Simple:

> Put every mistake on paper—as a one-sentence advice.

As explained in Rule 8, write that sentence down in the notebook you use whenever you need to solve a problem (which, in my experience, happens at least once a month). You will thereby be automatically reminded of the wisdom notes you wrote in the past, about both your own mistakes and other people's mistakes.

RULE 21

in a Pearl Shell

Learning from Your Own Mistakes Is Good,

Learning from Other People's Mistakes Is Even Better!

It's Smarter to Use a Scientifically Tested Medicine, Than to Try an Experimental One

- Learning from Your *Own Mistakes* Is Good—*but Painful*
- Learning from the *Mistakes of Others* Is Even Better—*and Painless*
- *Write Every Mistake in Your Notebook,* and Review Regularly

WHEN OTHER PEOPLE TRUST YOU, BE HONORABLE,

BUT WHEN YOU TRUST OTHER PEOPLE, BE CAREFUL!

Trust Is Tricky

WHEN OTHER PEOPLE TRUST YOU

Your "Yes" Is Your Oath

"To be trusted is a greater compliment than being loved," wrote author George MacDonald.

Indeed, being trusted is a singular honor. It's a sign of a person's utmost confidence in you.

And when other people trust you, you have a comprehensive responsibility toward them.

This responsibility involves your actions, your words, and even your thoughts concerning them.

Revere the trust that people place in you, and never ever break it. You can't squander this trust or take it lightly. Nor can you back out on it or violate it.

It takes years to build trust, and mere seconds to tear it down.

When to Sit Down, and When to Run

When people place their trust in you, you owe them nothing—unless and until you accept their trust.

It's a big decision.

It's like a contract. *You should think twice before signing on the dotted line.* Because if you do, you automatically accept the responsibility that comes with it.

Therefore:

**When you're approached for help, advice, or a favor
—by someone you don't know well—
hesitate!**

Take a pause. Be calculating about it before giving an answer. You can accept or reject that person's trust, or you could decide to accept it but limit your involvement.

If the person is someone you truly care for, you will probably agree to help. And with that, you acknowledge the heavy commitment that goes with it.

However:

> **If your instincts tell you to avoid this person altogether— then . . . RUN!**

You don't owe anyone an immediate response. Excuse yourself from the situation.

> **Simply say, "I'll think about it."**

Detach and delay!

Don't Be an Iscariot

With trust comes the obligation of integrity, reliability, and most important, loyalty.

It isn't always easy for people to place their trust in someone else. So, respect that. Treat other people's trust like precious porcelain, something to be handled with care.

Don't be like Judas Iscariot, the apostle who betrayed the trust of his leader, Jesus. Never violate a person's trust with any kind of disloyalty. Avoid all dishonorable behaviors, from the snide remark behind a person's back to overt disrespect. Nothing can be more painful to the people who trust you than to be betrayed by you.

When other people put their trust in you, behaving in a dignified and responsible way is the only way to go.

Your honor and reputation depend on it.

Your "Word" Is a Signed Contract

Your word matters, even for seemingly unimportant commitments.

Let's say you promise to pick up your friend's son from school at 4 p.m. Yet, you allow yourself to fall behind schedule and don't show up until 4:30 p.m. While standing in front of the school waiting for you, that unattended child could wind up in trouble. This is a careless violation of trust, perhaps without serious consequences in most cases, but nonetheless, unacceptable.

Your word is your bond.

If you make a promise, it's as if you signed a legal document—it isn't negotiable or breakable. And if it's broken, your honor is damaged with it. No excuse or apology will repair it.

So:

**Never promise unless you can deliver—
and always deliver whatever you promise.**

As Napoleon Bonaparte advised, "The best way to keep one's word is *not to give it!*"

The Prince of Egypt

In October of 1187, Saladin, an Egyptian sultan, conquered Jerusalem and took it from the Crusaders.

But amazingly, even after he defeated his Western enemies, Saladin remained admired and respected by them rather than despised.

Why? Because unlike other victorious leaders of his time, Saladin *kept his word.*

He promised, even before his victory, that he would treat the Christian women and children of Jerusalem with the utmost courtesy. And he did just that.

In his book *Primal Leadership*, author Daniel Goleman explains that the monarch "knew what he was doing, and why." For Saladin, keeping his promise wasn't just *honorable* but also *smart:* it was a way to earn people's trust.

Keeping your word keeps other people trusting you. "Losers make promises they often break. Winners make commitments they always keep," noted motivational speaker Denis Waitley.

Be a winner!

BUT WHEN YOU TRUST OTHERS

Trust Isn't Faith

Confusing trust with faith is a huge error but a very common one. The difference between the two is substantial.

> **Trust requires proof—whereas faith is blind.**

Faith is like a blank check. It requires nothing. It demands no validation and zero evidence, yet it grants 100 percent unquestioned belief. Faith should be reserved for things that are supernatural, such as religions and deities.

Trust, on the other hand, is like a certified check. It's issued based on an established account balance behind it. And it requires time, often years, to build.

So, don't confuse trust with faith: *Faith is holy, trust is not.*

> **Never give trust a blank check—**
> **not for anyone, not for any entity.**

Trust but Verify

Trust often isn't reciprocal.

For example, how many people have violated your trust in the past by being two-faced or indiscreet, repeating something you said in confidence just for the fun of gossiping? It's a hurtful experience.

Invest your trust carefully rather than casually. "Trust but verify," in the words of a Russian proverb.

Verify everything—before trusting anything.

It's All About Time

Trust shouldn't be blind. Its trustworthiness needs to be proven with words and deeds.

Trust isn't given away. It's earned, and it's earned . . . with time.

Trusted relationships with people should be like trusted relationships with institutions such as banks and courts of law: you would only trust one that has a solid history of proving itself over time.

Only time can supply us with proofs, and deliver to us enough insights and facts to justify our trust. Often, such evidence is slowly accumulated over years of dealing with an individual or an institution, or hearing about that person or that organization's stellar reputation.

Therefore:

Trust is time-based.

And it needs to be validated by passing through the "Test of Time."

The "Test of Time"

This test consists of two important stages.

- *The Time Period that "Precedes" an Interaction with a Person or an Institution*

  When we have known certain people for many years, such as family members, lifelong friends, a childhood housekeeper, or a special family doctor, they have proved themselves worthy of our trust. We imbue these people with trust because of the strong bond that's already established. Their track record is solid.

The same applies to institutions that, over time, have built a reputation of integrity and reliability, such as some charities, professional associations, and law enforcement agencies.

- *The Time Period that "Follows" an Interaction with a Person or an Institution*

As we deal with people and businesses unknown to us, we are continually assessing their treatment of us. Whether at a hospital, a school, or a clothing store, we keep our antennae up.

As we get to know these people and institutions better and build a record of proof, we decide whether they merit our trust or not. We only grant it after a period of time, whether it's weeks, months, or years.

The "Trust Elevator"

Imagine your trust as a ten-story building with an elevator!

Your trust is equally distributed at the rate of 10 percent per floor. So, the higher the elevator goes, the higher your cumulative level of trust.

Someone you just met, whom you know nothing about, starts off with a trust score of zero. He or she will be waiting for the elevator at the lobby!

As time passes, people who have proved themselves to you, such as family members, friends, service providers, and business partners; or institutions such as schools, corporations, associations, hospitals, or law firms, are elevated to higher levels, one floor at a time.

Some might wind up on floor 5 or 6. Others may even make it all the way to floor 8 or 9.

But no one gets to floor 10, the penthouse!—the 100 percent trust level.

Why not? Because:

We are all human—and as such—we are all vulnerable.

Even our most trusted family members and closest friends are vulnerable human beings, just as we are. If one day they become exposed to unexpected devastating health tragedies that erode their physical and psychological well-being, or if they become the victims of heartbreaking unforeseen social turmoil or calamitous financial misfortune, or if they simply suffer from side effects of advancing age, then their personalities, values, and rational reasoning could become impaired and falter—*and with it their commitment to us.*

The same principle applies to trusted and established professions and institutions. Even the largest banks may crash. Even century-old corporations can go belly-up. Even the most revered brands may turn insolvent. Some of the most trusted and established professionals— physicians, nurses, judges, soldiers, university professors—may not be dependable and ethical. Most of them are, but some aren't.

When it comes to trust:

> **No human being or institution can be 100% consistent,**
> **with a 100% trust level,**
> **that's 100% guaranteed—**
> **for life.**

So, your trust elevator should take its time—big-time!

You need a lethargic trust elevator. And don't allow it to ever reach the penthouse!

Occasionally, your trust elevator may even need to reverse course and head back down to a lower floor or to the lobby. This can happen when a person's trustworthiness is cast into doubt for whatever reason, or when you realize that some institutions don't deserve your confidence.

The "Triple Trust Traps"

Most of us make the mistake of awarding trust to other people from the very first encounter. We allow them to get onto our trust elevator when they should have been left in the basement!

By trusting too early and too quickly, we allow ourselves to be fooled.

This is especially true when it comes to what I call the "Triple Trust Traps," represented by the dollar sign, the heart symbol, and the caduceus.

In other words:

**The "Triple Trust Traps"
are the triad of money, love, and health.**

- *We Shouldn't Trust "Money-Related" Promises Too Quickly*
Greed can tempt us to put our trust in unethical investments and ruinous scams.
- *We Shouldn't Trust "Love-Related" Promises Too Quickly*
Romantic fantasies may seduce us, too early in the game, into ... *believing the beloved!* This can lead to intense disappointment, a broken heart or, even worse, a dangerous or abusive relationship.
- *We Shouldn't Trust "Health-Related" Promises Too Quickly*
We may fall prey to swindlers who sell magical recipes: promising potions for our ailments, alluring treatments for our looks, and fascinating elixirs for our longevity, most of which don't work.

With so much at stake, we should be shrewd and check all the facts before awarding our trust to a person or an institution.

As humorist Finley Peter Dunne advised, "Trust everybody, but cut the cards!"

Costly Letterheads

When I was starting my cosmetic surgery practice, Adam, a young man in his early thirties, came to see me for a rhinoplasty. He wanted to fix a nasal bump.

During the consultation, I carefully explained the procedure to Adam and showed him the expected result on a computer. Adam, who struck me as a pleasant and outgoing individual, was excited about having the surgery done and booked the procedure on the spot.

As per our usual protocol, Adam had to go through preoperative testing and photographs. When Lauren, our clinic manager, brought up the subject of payment, Adam informed her that his boss had offered to pay for his surgery as a gesture of appreciation for his valued contribution to the success of the company.

Adam's boss called Lauren that same afternoon and confirmed that he would pay all expenses. He gave Lauren his company phone number and address. He also promised that he would have a certified check for the total amount issued one week before the surgery, as requested by Lauren. In addition, he told her that the company would send a formal letter to our clinic confirming that it would cover Adam's fees.

Indeed, this letter arrived in the mail two days later. It was printed on proper letterhead and showed that the company operated in the import-export field. And it bore the name of the president, as well as the business phone number and address. All looked fine.

But when the check for the payment didn't arrive three days before the operation, Lauren called the company. A receptionist answered and asked her to hold for a minute while she transferred the call to the president, who then reassured Lauren that the check would be signed, certified, and delivered that very same day.

When the check still didn't show up as promised, Lauren called back. The president asked to speak to me directly. "Trust me, Doctor," he said. "I wrote the check, but I thought it would be safer if Adam delivered it to you in person on the day of his surgery. Trust me. You will have your money."

On the day of the procedure, Adam came with a check. It had the name of the company printed in its upper left corner and showed an account number at the Royal Bank of Canada, one of the most reputable banks in the country. It also had the company president's name on it.

But the check wasn't certified. When Lauren questioned Adam regarding this, he told her that the president didn't have time to go to the bank to certify it. Lauren came to see me, wondering if we should proceed with the operation. She warned me that an uncertified check might bounce.

But I reassured her that I wasn't worried because we had the signed letter from the company, including all the contact details. I also told Lauren that the president repeated to me twice, "Trust me"!

The surgery went fine. Adam's nose ended up nicely shaped.

A week later, Adam had an appointment with me to remove the cast, but he didn't show up. When Lauren called his phone number at home, there was no answer. She then called the company. There was no answer there either, despite the fact that it was a weekday. When we checked out the company name with the chamber of commerce, we found out that no such company existed.

A few days later, we received a call from our bank informing us that the check from Adam's purported company was rejected. We were told that the account had only been opened six weeks earlier and was closed a day after the operation took place. Plus, the account was always kept empty.

Needless to say, I never saw my money! Too bad I didn't know then what makeup artist Michelle Phan recommended, "Don't trust everyone, especially if they say *trust me!*"

What's extraordinary about this story is the lengths to which Adam went to get his surgery done for free. He installed and paid for two phone lines, one for his supposed home and the other for a fake company, he arranged for his friends to play the roles of president and receptionist, he opened a bank account and ordered checks, and he left the account open and empty until his ploy was complete.

It's amazing how pitiful but cunning dishonest people can be— how far they will go with their deceit and how effective they can be at playing the *trust me* game. All Adam's intricate, time-consuming maneuvers were made to save a few thousand dollars.

Can you imagine what a scoundrel would do for a scheme involving millions of dollars?

Here comes the answer.

Catch Me If You Can

Have you seen the movie *Catch Me If You Can*, starring Leonardo DiCaprio?

It's a true story based on the written memoir of Frank Abagnale Jr. As a sixteen-year-old, Abagnale ran away from home and successfully pulled off cons worth millions of dollars. Along the way, he proved himself to be a master at gaining other people's trust.

For example, while he was still in his teens, he decided to pretend to be a pilot.

He called Pan Am airlines and claimed to be a pilot who had lost his uniform. What did the Pan Am office staffer do? Did he ask Frank questions? Did he insist on some proof of identity? Not at all. Instead, whoever it was immediately arranged to supply him with what was supposedly a replacement uniform. Abagnale then used it to hop on a number of flights, traveling free of charge for hundreds of thousands of miles and enjoying free hotel rooms on his supposed layovers. Taking advantage of the trusting nature of the people around him, he socialized with his pilot colleagues in the cockpit and didn't spare the flight attendants from his conquests.

He then decided to play a lawyer.

He forged a Harvard law degree and even managed to land a job at the office of the Louisiana state attorney general. Amazing!

He next opted to play a doctor.

He was so trusted by the medical staff where he worked that he ended up supervising medical students at a nearby hospital! An incredible feat of charlatanism.

Finally, when Abagnale was caught and jailed, he still managed to escape. When he was recaptured, the FBI, impressed by his extraordinary resourcefulness, offered him his freedom on the condition that he help them identify other scams. He happily accepted.

Crooks and swindlers thrive on gullible people. Frank Abagnale was a crook extraordinaire. *But the main reason for his success lay with his victims, who trusted him too early and too quickly.*

They allowed their trust elevator to take him straight up to the . . . penthouse!

RULE 22

in a Pearl Shell

When Other People Trust You, Be Honorable, But When You Trust Other People, Be Careful!
Trust Is Tricky

When *Other People* Trust You
- *If Your Instincts Tell You to Run ... RUN!*
  Simply Say, "I'll Think About It."

But When *You* Trust Others
- *Your Yes Is Your Oath,* and *Your Word Is Your Bond*
- *Never Promise* Unless You Can Deliver, and *Always Deliver*
  Whatever You Promise
- *Don't Be an Iscariot*—Never Betray the People Who Trust You
- *Faith Is Holy, Trust Is Not*
- *Never Ever Give Trust a Blank Check*
  And Make Sure You *Cut the Cards*!
- *Trust Is Time-Based*
- *Your Trust Elevator Should Take Its Time—Big Time*
  It Should Never Reach Floor 10, the Penthouse!
- Beware of the *Triple Trust Traps:*
  Money, Love, and Health

DON'T GET EVEN, GET SMART!

*Do What's Best for You,
Not What's Best for Your Anger*

The "Fruit Basket" Phenomenon

Throughout life, you're destined to encounter individuals who are hostile to you.

These people can be highly critical, aggressive, dishonest, disloyal, greedy, or just plain evil. They may derive a certain pleasure from seeing you hurt, degraded, deflated, defeated, and even abused. And they will inevitably betray you, cheat you, steal money from you, or cause you harm in one way or another.

Here is a law of nature:

> There is always a bad apple—in every fruit basket.

This bad apple may be well hidden among the perfectly ripe oranges, apricots, and strawberries.

Likewise, in every group of people, there is always a troublesome soul, a bad apple of sorts, though his or her rotten side may be concealed behind a seductive facade. That's why you might be duped and miss the decay inside the apple until you've swallowed a bite of it. There it lurks—and there it hurts.

So, you need to be extra careful in order not to fall victim to rotten individuals.

If you're a high achiever who possesses wealth, status, or a good reputation, you're significantly more likely to be taken advantage of because your success ignites jealousy and greed in the bad apples.

The Boomeranger

When you've been cheated, defrauded, swindled, deceived, violated, or lied to, isn't your first reaction to get even?

It's only natural. You immediately focus on one goal—revenge.

You want the culprit to pay a price. And you self-righteously believe that revenge will deliver justice, thereby making you feel better.

In other words, you want to act upon your anger, in the erroneous belief that:

What's bad for the offender—is good for you.

It never is!

> **The flames of rage will consume you first . . .**
> **before they reach your enemy.**

Retaliation will only eat you up inside. You will be the first one to pay the price. It's like a boomerang—or, as I like to call it, a boomer-*anger*—that strikes back at you.

The heaviest thing you can carry is a grudge.

And grudges take a deep psychological and physical toll—your anxiety mounts, your emotions boil over, your blood pressure rises, your heart vessels contract, and your stomach burns.

All that venom leaves you in a state of aggravation and poor health. "When we hate our enemies, we are giving them power over us: power over our sleep, our appetites, our health and our happiness. Our enemies would dance with joy if only they knew how they were worrying us, lacerating us, and getting even with us," wrote the great Dale Carnegie.

As an old adage says:

> **Seeking revenge is like swallowing poison . . .**
> **and expecting the other person to die from it!**

Don't allow other people to poison your days. Although it may be tempting as a quick emotional fix, it will more often than not bring about only temporary relief, which is usually followed by long-term agony.

And revenge can spawn an endless cycle of retribution.

Looking Out for #1

What should you do when you're filled with rage? Retaliation may feel good in the moment, but it isn't good for you.

What you need to do first is look after what's best for you.

In other words:

Look out for #1—YOU!

"Looking out for number one is a conscious effort of doing the things that are good for you, those acts that would enhance your happiness and well-being," advised motivational speaker Robert J. Ringer.

Therefore, your goal, first and foremost, is to:

**Focus on what's good for you—
not on what's bad for your enemy.**

What's good for you isn't to make the offender pay for his or her offense. It isn't to insist that justice must be done. And isn't to do everything you can to end up the winner. It's none of the above. It isn't a duel.

Instead:

Use your brain—rather than your emotions.

By evaluating the situation intelligently and maintaining your objectivity, you improve your odds of coming out of any unfair situation with the best possible outcome—for you.

If this means not getting even with the jerk or the crook, so be it.

Winning a Scar

Scott, a homeowner, catches a knife-wielding thief in his home at night.

He is enraged and fights with the intruder, rather than allowing him to take what he wants and leave. During their altercation, the robber winds up stabbing Scott in the face, leaving him with a long, deep cut. In self-defense, Scott pulls out a gun and kills the intruder.

In hindsight, who do you think is the bigger loser of the two: the dead and buried thief or the alive and well but disfigured Scott?!

As far as Scott is concerned, the thief's death is no consolation to him whatsoever. He will have a hideous, conspicuous scar on his face for the rest of his life. And he carries the unsettling memory of having killed someone. What matters to Scott is his own welfare, not that of his aggressor.

Here is a favorite dictum of mine:

> **What happens to your enemy—**
> **is of negligible importance to you—**
> **however major it is.**
>
> **But what happens to you—**
> **is of major importance to you—**
> **however negligible it is!**

A Bumpy Ride

One day about eight years ago, I was driving home from the office on a highway that was unexpectedly jammed. The traffic was bumper to bumper as a result of a car accident a mile ahead.

As I approached the bottleneck point, a young driver in a red Mustang started impatiently honking his horn behind me, even though he could see there was no possible way for me to move any faster or out of his way.

As I was about to pass the area of the accident and drive into the clear highway, the Mustang driver hit the gas and cut in front of me. In the process, he smashed into the front left corner of my car, leaving my vehicle with a sizable gash and a broken headlight.

I was furious. I thought, *What a crazy guy. How can anyone be so inconsiderate?*

However, just before I got out of my car to confront this nutty character and let loose a stream of invective on him, I remembered my own rule and asked myself, *What's good for me here?*

I realized, in a flash, that venting my rage at this rude stranger wouldn't do me any good. I would become more aggravated for nothing. And given his aggressive driving, confronting him might even put me in physical danger. He could be just a careless driver, but he also could be a deranged lunatic or even a criminal. He could also be carrying a gun or knife. I made all these calculations in seconds, and found myself calming down right away!

Once I analyzed the situation and focused on what was good for me, I identified my two main goals: *getting home safely, and getting my car repaired promptly.*

As the Mustang driver emerged from his car, he had an insolent look in his eyes and loudly tried to put the blame on me for just "sitting there, not moving." I calmly replied that we should both recount our versions of what happened to the police and allow our insurance companies to deal with the matter. I defused his anger with my calm, nonconfrontational approach. Surprised by my reaction, he agreed.

Forty minutes later, I arrived home safely. I made a point of not making a big deal of the accident or of the damage to the car. *After all, the incident was just a little tempest in a little teapot (Rule 9), an incident I wouldn't remember six months down the road.*

Later that week, my insurance company decided that the accident wasn't my fault and handled the matter appropriately with the other driver's insurance company. And a week later, the car was back in my driveway, good as new.

In my mind, the whole drama was already forgotten. And throughout this unpleasant episode, I didn't suffer any minor or major physical harm, nor did I lose sleep or develop a stomach ulcer. It all ended fine.

But most important, my top priority was achieved: #1 was preserved!

Therefore, never be tempted to quench your thirst for revenge.

Don't get even—get even better!

RULE 23

in a Pearl Shell

Don't Get Even, Get Smart!
Do What's Best for You, Not What's Best for Your Anger

- *Seeking Revenge Is Like Swallowing a Poison* ... and Expecting the Other Person to Die from It!
- *The Flames of Rage Consume You First*, Before Reaching Your Enemy
- *Focus on What's Good for You—Not on What's Bad for Your Enemy*
- *What Happens to Your Aggressor* Is of Negligible Importance to You—However Major It Is,
  But What Happens to You Is of Major Importance to You—However Negligible It Is!
- *Look Out for #1—YOU*
- *Don't Get Even—Get Even Better!*
  Use Your *Brain*, Not Your *Emotions*

ALWAYS HAVE
A SAFETY NET—
JUST IN CASE!

The Wisdom of Plan B

It's a Big Deal, but No Big Deal

As we go through life, every one of us makes plans.

We decide *where* we want to go, *what* we want to do, and *whom* we want to be with. It's a grand plan for the trajectory of our lives. And we always imagine exactly what it will be like when we finally arrive.

But the best-laid plans can go awry. Oftentimes, things just don't turn out the way we expect. In fact, things rarely turn out exactly as we plan them.

"Man plans; God laughs!" notes a Yiddish proverb.

We all have a great-looking plan A, our ideal vision of the way things should be, even if it isn't always realistic. But when that plan suddenly goes off course and requires an immediate replacement, we need a solid plan B waiting in the wings.

Even if plan B isn't as good as plan A, having it at the ready gives us a sense of security and confidence in the future. It's our contingency plan, a vital one that can save us.

When you have got a lot at stake in terms of your family life, career or financial matters, wouldn't it be comforting to know that you always have a back-up strategy?

So, when something is a big deal in your life, having an alternative will make all the difference if your original hopes are dashed.

If this happens, it's no big deal!

With a plan B, you're like a circus performer who has a safety net under him, and a rope attached firmly to his belt. If he misses the catch, it doesn't mean the end of his life. With those safety measures in place, he has a safe alternative, a plan B.

The "Just in Case" Formula

In 1979, a band of twenty young performers started a street-theater group in Baie-Saint-Paul, a small town in Quebec.

They created intriguing, colorfully dressed fantastical characters who danced, played music, juggled, walked on stilts, and breathed fire. And they called themselves *Cirque du Soleil*.

Since then, this so-called "circus of the sun" has become a huge phenomenon, a global leader in live acrobatic entertainment. That's a sizable achievement in and of itself.

But what's more amazing about Cirque du Soleil is its extraordinary safety record. Employing some four thousand people and 1,300 artists, and with tens of thousands of shows presented in 450 cities in more than 60 countries around the world, Cirque du Soleil did not incur a single fatal accident on stage during its initial thirty-year history.

How did the organization manage such an unbelievable accomplishment?

At its international headquarters and training camps in Montreal, Cirque du Soleil assembled its greatest thinkers and commissioned them to put together a master safety plan. The result was an extraordinarily meticulous set of guidelines that assured the maximum possible protection for the performers.

These safety measures were based on the "Just-in-Case" formula.

For example, if a harness breaks down or a wire malfunctions, a fail-safe mechanism is in place to lower the performer safely to the stage—*just in case*. During stunts, performers wear earpieces to guarantee that they clearly hear safety cues—*just in case*. Special airbags are placed on top of the safety nets to further buttress the protection for artists who fall from heights of up to seventy feet. Furthermore, these airbags can inflate and deflate independently. And if a power outage occurs, each of those airbags has its own power supply—*just in case*.

In other words, Cirque du Soleil had a plan B for every move, every fall, and every equipment concern.

The "Just-in-Case" formula has worked marvelously for Cirque du Soleil in its first thirty years. It can do the same for you.

**You're in great shape when you have a plan B . . .
and in great trouble when you don't.**

One Option Isn't an Option

"Don't put all your eggs in one basket," as the saying goes.

So, for example:

- *Avoid Depending Solely on One "Job"*

No matter how great that job of yours may be, marshaling a plan B may sometimes be essential.

If your company shows signs of instability, or makes a change in hiring and firing practices, you should have your résumé prepared or already in circulation—*just in case*. If layoffs and buyouts ever do begin, you will have your plan B ready.

- *Avoid Depending Solely on One "Person"*

When you're too reliant upon a particular individual, such as a doctor, a housekeeper, a friend, or a neighbor, you're making yourself vulnerable. You need a number of people to whom you can turn in a crisis.

For example, if you employ a person who is indispensable to you, such as a caregiver or babysitter, consider hiring two part-time individuals for the job. It won't cost any more and you'll have a backup—*just in case* one becomes ill or decides to quit. Likewise, if you're unhappy in a business relationship, start planning an exit strategy or looking for another option—*just in case*.

Having that kind of backup even applies to friends. If you want to go to the movies or out for dinner and one friend drops out, isn't it great to know that you have somebody else to call?

- *Avoid Depending Solely on One "Choice"*

As in life, avoid depending solely on one option in business or investments.

For example, if most of your savings are in the stock market, diversify by relocating some funds into safer positions. They might be less exciting in terms of monetary gains but may be more reliable—*just in case*.

An Operating Room with a Safety Net

My surgical center has a well-equipped operating room.

For all my surgeries large and small, *I don't use general anesthesia.* Instead, I implemented a sophisticated approach in which I administer local anesthesia along with a special efficient type of sedation. It's a personal preference. It allows patients to be fully sleeping and completely pain-free during surgery, but still breathing on their own, without being intubated.

In the operating room, we have multiple sophisticated monitors that allow us to follow, on screens, all kinds of vital signs, including oxygen saturation, blood pressure, heart rate, respiration, body temperature, and so forth. We also have a system in which sensitive electrodes are placed over the forehead to monitor and precisely evaluate the depth of sedation during the procedure. It can even detect instantly if the sleeping patient starts to feel pain!

In addition, our operating room follows a special two-for-one concept: for every piece of equipment, there is a backup.

In other words, everything is doubled.

Therefore, there are two monitors to check blood oxygenation, as well as two for everything else. So, for example, if a patient moves a hand in such a way as to detach the sensitive oxygen electrode, the backup electrode on the other hand will still be functioning.

Also, every surgical instrument or other piece of equipment has an identical double, in case of loss or breakage.

This is our plan B for the operating room: We have a safety net for every item—just in case.

This duplication concept also applies to personnel. Every nurse and technician in the operating room has a backup, just in case he or she cannot make it to work.

This concept even applies to me! Dr. Amanda Fanous, a competent successful surgeon and a university teacher, who also happens to be my daughter! and partner, can fill in for me—*just in case!*

RULE 24

in a Pearl Shell

Always Have a Safety Net—Just in Case!
The Wisdom of Plan B

- *Don't Put All Your Eggs in One Basket*
  In Life, Things May Not Turn Out the Way You Expect
- *When Something Is a Big Deal for You,* Always Have a Safety
  Net—*Just in Case!*
- *You're in Great Shape* When You Have a Plan B,
  And in *Great Trouble* When You Don't Have One

APPEARANCE COUNTS

*For You, and Everyone,
and Everything Around You*

Dressed and Groomed

In our culture, appearance is the way you present yourself to the world. It's the first thing people see. And they judge you immediately by it.

When you get up in the morning and prepare for the day, what do you typically do to put yourself together? Most of us take a shower, attend to our hair, and then choose an outfit. A trivial routine? A superfluous custom? No, it's essential.

> **What you look like—**
> **determines how the world will perceive you.**

No wonder it's so valued in show business, politics, and all other human interactions.

Nonverbal cues, communicated visually, influence your fortunes in life. It's been proven that when we meet someone, we decide if he or she is confident, trustworthy, competent, or likable within a fraction of a second. Before the hellos, a decision has already been made.

Having an attractive general appearance—being well groomed and well dressed—automatically impresses people. Eleanor Roosevelt, for example, was one of the world's most admired women. She may not have been a classic beauty, but her overall appearance was always impeccable, bolstered by her poise and dignity.

> **Your general appearance has a powerful impact on others—**
> **the same way their appearance has an impact on you.**

So, make the effort to look your very best, every single day.

Proper hair styling, and perhaps coloring, can greatly improve your looks. Your hairstyle frames your face, just as a good frame complements a painting.

Similarly, dressing smartly enhances your appearance, just as a nice wrapping enhances a gift. Elegant fashion in the right colors can make you appear years younger. And regardless of your choice of wardrobe, your clothing should always be impeccably neat and in good taste.

If you're a woman, consider wearing makeup, even in a subtle way. Women are lucky to have this option. It's one of the reasons they appear so much more attractive than men in weddings and formal photos. But don't wait for such a big occasion to look better. Foundation, blush, eye shadow, mascara, and lipstick, ideally of the organic varieties, can make a woman look more attractive and younger. Even a faint application can make a difference.

Finally, smiling is a universal signal of warmth and approachability that enhances attractiveness. Smiling also makes you look younger because it raises and fills your cheeks, taking years off your face.

All these simple tricks can lift your looks—without a face-lift!

At Work and Off Work: What Works?

If you want to look like the credible accountant, lawyer, businessperson, schoolteacher, or executive chef that you are, dress like one.

As author Bianca Frazier noted:

> **"Dress how you want to be addressed!"**

Your attire should follow the traditions and changing norms of your profession. You have a role to play, and you need to play it to a tee. That includes wearing the right clothes and grooming yourself well.

Would you trust a doctor attired in shorts, sandals, and a tank top? I don't think so. You would rather place your physical well-being in the hands of a physician dressed in a suit and a crisp white medical coat.

Likewise, would you want to eat food prepared by a chef wearing a visor and a T-shirt? Or would you want to taste a repast prepared by a chef dressed in an impeccable white jacket, complete with a toque blanche on his or her head?

Even outside of work, you should dress appropriately for all social occasions, formal or casual. How often have you gone to a wedding or a christening and been shocked by the one person who shows up in tennis shoes? On the other hand, if you wear a suit and tie on a cruise during the day, you sure will look out of place.

It's essential to dress well and appropriately for every outing and occasion. You never know whom you will meet there.

And you wouldn't want to ruin that important first impression.

Even Your Surroundings Count

The physical space around you, at work or at home, also affects the way people perceive and judge you.

For example, a neat, professional-looking desk at work makes a positive impression on your colleagues and clients. It conveys the idea that you're organized and meticulous in your affairs.

Conversely, a sloppy living room filled with dirty clothes, old pizza boxes, and empty beer cans conveys a negative message about your cleanliness and self-esteem to your friends.

Being orderly about your living and workspaces also has an impact on you. And a clean space allows you to keep your affairs organized and your mind clear.

Immaculate surroundings reduce your stress levels.

Bottom line: Your surroundings at work, at home, in the car and even in your gym locker all represent you.

They're part of the package!

The "Morning Mirror" Test

Looks are the physical part of our appearance. And they are much more complex to analyze and explain than you might initially think.

Let me start by asking you a simple question:

How do you feel when you look at yourself in the mirror each morning?

Nothing is more revealing than this daily encounter with your reflection.

If you feel good or even neutral about the way you look, great! There is no problem. You appreciate and accept the fact that you look exactly the way God created you. It's a blessing. Congratulations. You can happily skip the rest of this chapter.

However, if you feel dissatisfied looking into that mirror, keep reading. You're part of a reasonably good percentage of the population unhappy about their physical appearance.

In my cosmetic surgery practice, patients come to me with a great variety of complaints, including sagging jowls, wrinkles, droopy eyelids, oversize noses, flat chests, and body curves in the wrong places. This dissatisfaction often festers, eating away at their self-esteem.

We are often our own worst critics. Throughout our lives, we may at some point feel self-conscious and question the way we look. Are we too fat, too skinny, too old, too wrinkled, or too something else? Are we a little alarmed by those lines creeping in around our eyes and mouths? Or by the gray hair at our temples? Are we bothered by an obtrusive nose or baggy eyelids? Or do we dislike the loose skin and extra fat along our necks and tummies?

We may be asking ourselves, *Why aren't we better looking? Why is our body working against us? How can we look ten years younger?* And as we grow older, many of us realize that we look tired and sad when we're neither tired nor sad.

But at the same time, we may feel like it's vain to want to improve our looks. So, we suppress these negative thoughts.

We try to forget about our looks and just live with them.

Are You Vain? If Yes, You're Not Alone

Vanity seems to be such a frowned-upon attribute.

Vain people carry the stigma of being superficial, foolish and unworthy of serious endeavors. Society and tradition have made us believe that, to be respectable and dignified, we shouldn't be concerned about our looks.

Yet vanity is part of human nature. It's built into the human psyche.

We are all vain—but in different ways.

Some of us have the insight to recognize this and deal with it, while others of us let it affect us, making us self-conscious and hesitant. And some of us are courageous enough to admit it, but some are not.

All this self-doubt is unnecessary. After all, who among us doesn't want to look good? Why shouldn't a man or woman look as attractive as he or she possibly can?

While some people may not be vain about their appearance, they may be vain in other areas of their lives.

What do you call wearing designer brands and driving luxury cars? Vanity, of course.

And how different are these two persons: One woman undergoes a facelift in an effort to look more attractive, while the other applies full make-up, jewelry, perfume, and a fashionable hairstyle to . . . also look more attractive?!

Many of our so-called normal behaviors are nothing but disguised vanity.

It's all vanity, but in different forms.

The "Mars and Venus" Fallacy

Many people think that women are more vain than men. This isn't true.

The reality, which has been repeatedly confirmed to me over the course of my career, is that both men and women are vain, though in somewhat different ways.

Women traditionally care more about looks, jewelry, dresses, shoes, and perfumes.

Men are typically concerned about their apparent masculinity, their fitness levels, and the thickness of their hair. It may not be considered macho for men to care about the way they look, yet they still do. They also tend to be more preoccupied with status symbols such as cars, watches, clothes, and investment portfolios.

However, in the twenty-first century, these traditional male-female lines are becoming more and more blurred!

What Would You Do in Their Shoes?

Are you worried about other people's remarks on your new hairstyle or your recent Botox injection? Are you concerned that they may see you as vain or shallow?

If you feel this way, consider the following true examples of two patients from my practice.

The first patient, Olivia, is a fifty-year-old woman who wanted to have surgery for her drooping eyelids. She was accompanied to the consultation by her son, who thought she was foolish to contemplate such surgery. At the age of thirty, he didn't really know what aging is. To him, anyone over forty was too old to consider self-improvement. As he saw it, people in their fifties and sixties ought to just accept their fate. He felt it was ridiculous that his aged mother wanted to look more attractive. As far as he was concerned, she was fine as she was.

He didn't realize that Olivia, his mother, still had a life of her own, and that she still craved attention, intimacy, and love.

My second patient, Emma, is a young woman who had just turned twenty and wanted to have a rhinoplasty and a breast augmentation. She had asked her parents to help finance these procedures. But the parents regarded her desire as a sign of immaturity. They both agreed that Emma had a somewhat large nose and was a bit flat-chested, but so what? They loved their daughter as she was. Concerned about possible surgical complications, they felt that opposing these procedures was their parental duty.

What her parents failed to consider was that their daughter is part of a generation that significantly values looks in a culture that facilitates comparisons all the more readily through social media. The parents had never faced the daily competition-and-comparison game that's played among college classmates nowadays. They didn't realize that Emma, who may have been still a kid in their eyes, had grown up and had a burning desire to be admired. They didn't appreciate how agonizing it is for a person of their daughter's age to have sleepless nights troubled by the insecurity she felt about her appearance. They couldn't understand that her generation was under enormous pressure to compete, to do better, and be better in every way—education, career, income . . . and looks.

They may not have understood this, but I did. And I succeeded in explaining it to them by encouraging them to imagine being in her shoes.

The "Looks and Lives" Phenomenon

As a surgeon who has dealt with tens of thousands of patients, I've seen with my own eyes the powerful impact that plastic aesthetic surgery has on so many lives.

I've witnessed innumerable cases of patients whose lives have been transformed once their appearance was changed for the better. They leaped from distress to elation, and from low self-esteem to restored confidence. The impact was not only psychological, but also crossed over into real-world experience.

> **Enhanced looks . . . enhance lives.**

Many of my patients witnessed *a reversal of fortune* in their lives.

Men and women in their twenties and thirties who had received little interest from the opposite sex were suddenly wildly pursued following a nose job, a liposuction, or a breast augmentation.

Married women with children who struggled for intimate attention from their busy husbands were once again desirable after a face-lift or a tummy tuck.

Divorced men, desperate to find the right mate, many of whom took their looks for granted during the years of their marriages, were reclaiming their luck after an eyelid surgery or a mini face-lift.

Aging workers who deal with the public, such as salespeople and receptionists—people who saw their careers threatened by a younger generation—were given a second chance after facial injections or skin treatments.

Even among celebrities, this beneficial impact is acknowledged. Jane Fonda once confided that her plastic surgery bought her an additional decade in Hollywood, with loads of job offers.

To put it simply:

> **Our looks affect everyone else—**
> **just as everyone else's looks affect us.**

After film stars, no one is more conscious of physical appearance than politicians. What do you think a politician needs to have in order to persuade people to vote for her or him? Brains? Experience? Honesty? Leadership?

All these are essential. However, likability is probably the biggest factor. And part of a politician's appeal is his or her looks. Most voters aren't well versed in foreign policy and economics. Most have no opportunity to meet the candidates in person, check their credentials or evaluate their work ethic. So, how do they choose their political leaders? They do it mostly based on what they see on television: the way politicians talk, the way they act, and the way they look.

John F. Kennedy, one of the most popular American presidents in history, realized the power that looks can carry, and further enhanced his by keeping himself well-groomed at all times.

The Goodness Meter

"It's amazing how complete is the delusion that beauty is goodness," Russian novelist Leo Tolstoy once said.

Indeed, studies have shown that beautiful people are treated more favorably. "Good-looking men and women are generally judged to be more talented, kind, honest and intelligent than their less attractive counterparts," according to Dr. Gordon Patzer, a specialist in the effects of physical attractiveness.

Even royalty agreed. "A good face is the best letter of recommendation," decreed the sixteenth-century Queen Elizabeth I.

So, here is another one of my dictums in life:

> People are judged by their looks—
> just as a book is judged by its cover.

Does It Pay?

Beauty and youth are interdependent, as both project the ideals of health and success. Given that, one might wonder whether good looks deliver financial rewards too.

The ugly truth is that—they do!

Even though it might sound shallow, and some people won't admit it, physical attractiveness not only leads to more opportunities for romantic love and friendship, but also increases the chances of advancement in the workplace.

Economists at the University of Texas at Austin, led by Daniel Hamermesh, conducted surveys to determine the correlation between beauty, income, and happiness. They pointed out that attractive people are happier, tend to make more money, and pair off with more attractive spouses.

What Comes First … Ranks First

First impressions really do count when it comes to initial encounters, such as dates, job interviews and social gatherings.

Within less than a second of meeting a stranger, we decide, wrongly or rightly, whether that person is intelligent, successful, charming, dour, aggressive, introverted, trustworthy or suspicious.

> Looks may be more crucial than personality—
> when meeting somebody *for the first time*.

And this first impression is extremely decisive as to whether or not we will give that stranger a chance to know us further!

What makes looks such a tipping point in first impressions? The answer is both interesting and commonsensical:

> **Looks are the easiest and fastest way
> to judge a stranger!**

Incorrect as it may be, it's quick and effortless, therefore tempting and practical.

It's amazing that we tend to make instant judgments about a person's personality, professional ability, and mood—just by looking at him or her. And that applies to many crucial occasions in life—a first date, a job interview, a business deal.

On the other hand, if we deal with people for months or years, we see them as they truly are.

Unfortunately, not every stranger gets the benefit of time. The sensible and proper thing to do when meeting someone for the first time is to at least delay our judgment until we get to know that person better. But we don't!

Unflattering looks will put us at a disadvantage with strangers we meet for the first time. Is it unfair? Perhaps, but it's also true.

Do You Look the Way You Feel?

Back to the mirror.

When you see your reflection, do you look the way you feel?

If the answer is *yes,* then you have no problem. You look authentic.

However, if the answer is *no,* then you have what's called a "false expression." It's understandable that you should look tired and sad when you're actually tired and sad. However, if you look sad or tired or angry or sleepy when you aren't, then you have a problem. You project an erroneous impression of yourself to other people.

Here is a story of mine.

When I started my cosmetic surgery practice, Cheryl, a patient in her early fifties, came to my office for a consultation.

As I saw her entering the exam room, I assumed she was there for a face-lift. But she wasn't. Her main complaint surprised me.

"Doctor, I look sad. Can you do something about it?"

As I examined Cheryl, I had to admit that her resting facial expression did look melancholic. I was bewildered. I had been fortunate enough to train in Boston with accomplished plastic surgeon Professor Richard Webster of Harvard University. I had learned from him how to modify faces, but not how to change expressions.

I re-examined Cheryl. I was baffled at first, but after some analysis of her face, I came to the conclusion that her sad look was primarily the result of her drooping eyebrows and the sagging angles of her mouth.

That day, I put my finger on an important issue in facial plastic surgery: *the false expression.* I spent the following year studying all kinds of facial expressions and ended up writing a scientific article about an innovative approach that I called "Expression Plasty"—the art of analyzing false expressions and designing ways to reverse them.

Since then, it has become obvious to me that when looking at a face, one shouldn't consider only features, but also, expressions.

Good Looks Aren't What You Think

In 2014, I was invited to be a guest speaker at an international cosmetic surgery conference in Las Vegas, where I gave a talk titled "What Is Beauty?"

My audience of plastic and cosmetic surgeons was expecting to hear me talk about the rules and mathematical principles behind physical attractiveness. Instead, what I related in my presentation shocked most of them.

"In his 1859 masterpiece, *On the Origin of Species*, Darwin explained that evolution is far from being an aimless process. Evolution, he posited, is focused on the perpetuation and reproduction of the human race by favoring fertility," I said.

Then I continued, "My question to you is: Is it a coincidence that men are attracted to women with high fertility chances—that is, women who are young, full-breasted (now we know why!), and have a small hip-to-waist ratio? And is it by chance that women are attracted to highly fertile males who are young, tall, and muscular, as well as rich and successful—in other words, men who can also protect their offspring and provide for them?"

I resumed, "Believe it or not, human beauty isn't the glamorous piece of art you thought it was. What makes people beautiful isn't mathematical perfection. They're beautiful simply because we perceive them as beautiful."

In other words:

> **"Human beauty is nothing more than a perception—
> and this perception is programmed by evolution."**

Then I concluded:

> **"What we see as beautiful—
> is what Nature wants us to see as beautiful!"**

Outside Versus Inside

Thanks to advances in medical care and better lifestyle choices, such as healthful eating and exercising, our overall life expectancy has increased.

This, however, has also created a problem.

> **Our bodies are kept relatively healthier and younger—
> but not our faces.**

This is because we are healthier and fitter than our parents and grandparents were.

Therefore, we may have a face that reflects our real age, while at the same time having a younger-looking body with the corresponding feelings and flare!

In other words, due to our improved physical fitness, *our faces don't keep up with our bodies.*

> **When we are forty or sixty,**
> **our faces also look forty or sixty...**
> **but not our bodies!**

Therefore, our apparent age may not match the way feel, or how physically and psychologically fit we actually are.

And that creates another problem.

As we grow older, there could be a disconnect between:

> **The way we look on the outside...**
> **and the way we feel on the inside!**

That's why many people choose cosmetic injections and surgery to obtain a face or a body that reflects their youthful inner state of body and mind.

Are Cosmetic Treatments Worth It for You?

There is a popular stereotype that people concerned with their looks or seeking aesthetic surgery are either movie stars or eccentric characters of some kind.

Totally untrue.

After many years of performing tens of thousands of cosmetic surgeries and administering many thousands of injections, I learned that most people seeking to improve their looks tend to be perfectionistic, ambitious, and courageous. And they come from all professions and all strata of society.

Are you a candidate for cosmetic injections or surgeries?

It all depends on your "Morning Mirror" test.

If you look in the mirror and feel fine about the way you look, then you obviously don't need anything done.

But if you feel a little unhappy with the way you look, then you might consider having minor interventions such as fillers or Botox injections. You could also be a candidate for a mild laser treatment or other noninvasive procedures.

However, if you feel quite unhappy with your looks, then you may contemplate having minimally invasive surgery, such as an eyelid lift, a liposuction, or a mini facelift.

Many of the innovative approaches that I wrote about in plastic surgery journals and taught at medical conferences involve mini-incisions and mini-dissection (limited surgery) techniques. "Less is more" has always been my motto for the entire spectrum of cosmetic surgery, including rhinoplasty, face-lifts, forehead lifts, and breast augmentations. Satisfactory, natural-looking results with fewer incisions, fewer risks, and faster recovery are what I always strive to achieve.

In general, advanced techniques and technologies in the field of plastic cosmetic surgery have greatly improved over the years and are continuously moving toward the ultimate goal of delivering even better results, with still fewer risks.

Beauty: Blessing or Curse?

"Beauty is the gift of God," Aristotle said.

It's true that physically attractive people *do* have it easier in life as we have seen. In that sense, beauty is a blessing.

You might then assume that those blessed beautiful people are always happy, and that their lives are one long voyage of sunshine, uninterrupted by clouds or rain.

However, I personally believe that beauty comes with a hefty price tag:

A curse called *"aging"!*

With age, the playing field begins to level out. Attractive people enjoy a number of advantages until aging starts to affect their natural assets. Like the careers of Olympic athletes, the free ride of good-looking people diminishes with age.

Beginning in their late thirties, attractive individuals often become distressed as the number of compliments they receive dwindles. This is especially true once they pass fifty. There was a time when they could walk into a room and garner admiring glances, but in later life they feel ignored, even invisible. What a change from what they experienced in their twenties.

As attractive people grow older, they start to experience a true reversal of fortunes—both in their physical condition and psychological health.

On the other hand, plainer looking individuals generally experience little distress related to their aging appearance.

So, here is another one of my dictums in life:

> **Beauty is like wealth—**
> **it's much easier to start poor and continue to live modestly,**
> **than to be rich one day and poor the next!**

RULE 25

in a Pearl Shell

Appearance Counts
For You, and Everyone, and Everything Around You

- *What You Look Like—Is How the World Perceives You*
- *Your Looks Affect Everyone Else*—Just as Everyone Else's Looks Affect You
- *People Are Judged by Their Looks*—Just as a Book Is Judged by Its Cover
- Even *Your Surroundings* Represent You
- Make the Effort to *Look Your Best* Every Single Day
- *Enhanced Looks . . . Enhance Lives*
- *What Comes First . . . Ranks First*
  Looks May Be More Crucial than Personality—When We Meet Someone for the First Time
- What We See as Beautiful—Is What Nature Wants Us to See as *Beautiful!*
- *Beauty Is a Blessing, But It Comes with a Curse Called "Aging"!*
- *With Age, Our Bodies May Be Relatively Young, While Our Faces Aren't*
  It's a Disconnect Between *Our Outside vs. Our Inside*
- And, by the Way, *How's Your "Morning Mirror" Test?!*

IF YOU FEEL UNBEATABLE, YOU ARE

Only YOU Can Lower Your Head!

The "Good Luck" Phenomenon

No matter how fortunate we are, and no matter how much good health, money or status we enjoy, one thing is for certain:

> **Good luck is never forever.**

Good luck is always preceded or followed by a period of misfortune.

We all go through difficult times—moments of disappointment and heartbreak that disrupt our plans and our lives. And these occasions remind us that we are vulnerable and fragile, both physically and psychologically.

Ironically, when we face such major setbacks, it's often the psychological impact that's more dangerous and debilitating than the physical one.

> **Our perception of a calamity—a mere thought—**
> **can make or break us.**

In other words:

> **Our well-being is mostly controlled from . . . within our heads!**

The problem isn't only the external event, but mostly our internal reaction to it.

The enemy lurks within!

The "Stain and Pain" Phenomenon

There are two basic types of misfortunes that haunt our psyches.

- *A Past Calamity*—which lingers like a stubborn stain.
- *A Present Calamity*—which induces acute pain.

PAST CALAMITIES

The Past Stain

A past calamity is an event from our past that has left a profound imprint.

It's a set-in emotional stain, a spot that just sits there inside us, indelibly, and won't go away. It's like an open wound, one that never heals.

A Stain Remover Called "Gone and Forgotten"

When stricken with a heavy misfortune, whether in the realm of health, wealth, family, or career, you might lose all hope.

And with your guard down, you continue feeling crushed, languishing in pain, and filled with regret and self-pity. *How could this have happened to me?* you keep wondering.

And your body language tells the whole story—you walk with your head down and your shoulders slumped, dragging your feet like a vanquished warrior.

Never dwell on the past.

Don't be your own worst enemy. Change your deadbeat attitude.

Your crumbled posture and shattered facial expression will tell the world you're a dud.
And the world will take your word for it!

Instead, when you've been beaten, pull yourself up and behave like a leader. You may have lost a battle, but you didn't necessarily lose the war.

Every problem under the sun is temporary. When you've been thrashed, humiliated, or defeated in the past—it's history. Forget it.

Blow up those past blows!

Make them gone and forgotten. If you don't, you'll cause nothing but misery for yourself and invite condescension from others. Some people will feel sorry for you, but others will have contempt for you.

**When you're *down*,
and when you walk bent *down*,
with your head *down*—
people will look *down* on you!**

So, shift up instead. How?
- First, *keep your head up*—literally.
- Second, *Stand Straight and Look Straight* (Rule 4).
- Third, *close down any negative discussion before it starts!* Drown those nosy questions with this one-liner, *"I don't want to talk about it."* Let rumors die and sarcasm suffocate at your feet.

Remember:

**Walk and behave like a loser . . .
and the whole world will treat you as one.**

**Walk and behave like a winner . . .
and people may doubt you at first
but will ultimately end up doubting themselves!**

The "Walk Like a Winner" Phenomenon
A few years ago, one of my colleagues, Dr. Reed, a Canadian facial plastic surgeon, went through a professional catastrophe.

He was the subject of a very unflattering newspaper article, filled with derisive and biased remarks by the reporter, who portrayed him as an unethical, money-hungry physician.

What made matters worse was the insultingly sarcastic tone of the article. The reporter maliciously quoted only parts of my friend's answers to some questions, leading the reader to come away with distorted opinions. Dr. Reed was understandably devastated.

A month later, I was at a medical conference at the New York's Waldorf Astoria hotel when I met Dr. Reed by chance in the elevator. I almost didn't recognize him. He looked like he had aged ten years and was obviously severely depressed. He had lost weight, which was very noticeable in his face, giving him sunken eyes.

I was shocked. I had always liked him as a person and admired him as a surgeon, so I invited him out for lunch.

As we sat down to eat, he started telling me about how unfortunate he was. I interrupted him right off the bat.

I told him that I had a little advice for him as a friend. "Don't worry about the past, and don't be perturbed by what other people think of you."

Then I told him what I just told you, "Walk as if you have nothing to hide. Walk like a winner, and others will believe you are." I added, "Put a big smile on your face, and nip any curious questions in the bud."

I didn't hear from Dr. Reed for the next five months. He then called my office and left a message saying that he was inviting me out for dinner on the first evening of an upcoming conference in Houston.

Three weeks later, as I arrived at the designated restaurant, Dr. Reed was waiting for me at our table with his wife by his side. He looked like a new man, so different from the pitiful mess I had seen just a few months earlier. He was beaming—as handsome and upbeat as he used to be prior to his setback.

He told me that, at first, he doubted my advice would help him. However, his wife, a pleasant and smart woman, encouraged him at least to give it a chance. He confessed that the first morning he tried it, he found it difficult. He felt weird. However, by the afternoon, he could already see a difference in the way he felt and the way other people interacted with him.

And by the second day, the change was like a miracle—his whole environment was back to what it had been before the setback.

The bad press was forgotten. It seemed to have just vanished!

CURRENT CALAMITIES

The Current Pain

A present calamity is one that's happening right now, unfolding in real time. It causes us to suffer and panic, or to feel discouraged and unstable, depending on the unpredictable evolving circumstances.

A Painkiller Called "Never Give In, Never Give Up"

Every group of people needs a leader.

A country needs a president, a prime minister, a king, a pharaoh, or a tsar. A family needs a patriarch, a matriarch, or a godfather. A tribe needs a chief. A class needs a teacher. A sports team needs a coach. A company needs a CEO. And a religious community needs a pope, a rabbi, an imam, a mullah, or a grand mufti.

Leaders are especially needed to guide and inspire people in difficult times. They make critical decisions, and with their iron will and unshakable faith in their ultimate triumph, they lead their followers to victory.

Do you know what's the most important difference between leaders and followers?

Great leaders keep fighting, and never give in or give up.

So, when facing dire situations in your own life, do what leaders do:

Never give in or give up.

The Man Who Beat Out
Shakespeare, Darwin, and the Queen

In a 2002 survey taken by the BBC, the British public was invited to choose the person they considered to be the greatest Briton of all time.

The list of one hundred names included, among others, Shakespeare, Darwin, and Queen Elizabeth I.

Guess who was voted the greatest of all Brits, ranking in the number one spot?

Sir Winston Churchill!

Churchill's tremendous leadership during World War II changed history. Brave, tireless, and bold, he exemplified extraordinary resolve as he stood up to the vicious aggression of Nazi Germany. And he was charismatic, fiery, witty, charming, and persuasive, all of which helped him achieve his goals.

Yet Churchill wasn't flawless or infallible. He made his share of missteps and mistakes.

Nevertheless, what made his leadership most invaluable to Britain was his inspiring determination and infectious defiance.

At a pivotal moment in history, when the British were frightened and discouraged, Churchill, with the sheer power of his personality, galvanized them to persist in their struggle and reassured them of ultimate victory. "Never, never, never, never give in," he shouted in his radio broadcasts.

Winston Churchill was *unbeatable* because he believed that nothing is impossible, and he *never gave in or gave up*.

When he passed away in 1965, Sir Arthur Bryant proclaimed, "The age of giants is over."

Indeed.

RULE 26

in a Pearl Shell

If You Feel Unbeatable, You Are
Only YOU Can Lower Your Head!

- *Good Luck Is Never Forever*
- Our Well-being Is Mostly Controlled from . . .
  within Our Heads!
- When Faced with Past Blows, *Blow Them Up!*
  Make Them *Gone and Forgotten*
- When Faced with Current Blows, *Be A Churchill!*
  Never, Never, Never *Give In* or *Give Up*
- *Walk and Behave Like a Loser* . . . and the Whole World Will
  Take Your Word for It!
  When You're *Down,* and When You Walk Bent *Down,* with
  Your Head *Down*—People Will Look *Down* on You!
- *Walk and Behave Like a Winner* . . . and Others Will Treat
  You as One. They May Doubt You at First, but Will End Up
  Doubting Themselves!

TODAY IS ALL YOU'VE GOT!

*It's the Only Live Movie
You Can Act In, Edit, and Enjoy;
Yesterday's Movie Can't Be Rewound,
and Tomorrow's Movie Isn't Out Yet!*

Movie Name: Today

Scene #1: *Opening Scene*

Think about this for a second: what happens when you're totally consumed by a movie, a book, a television show or a sporting event?

Time flies. Your worries and regrets vanish. Your problems seem to disappear—poof!

That's because you're fully present in the moment and can disengage from past and future concerns.

> **Concentrating on living every minute of your life—
> is a secret of joyful living.**

Yet, we are so often lost in the past, filled with regret and guilt, or obsessed with the future, worrying about what might happen tomorrow or the day after.

Meanwhile, the *now* is completely missed.

Yet, the only time you can live is *now!*

Today is the only day when you're actually breathing, moving, feeling, and thinking. All the other time periods exist only in your head. They aren't real.

You can't possibly live in the past. It's gone. It's history.

And you can't exist in the future either. It's not here yet. It's unknown, and its arrival isn't even guaranteed!

In other words:

> **Yesterday is history.
> Tomorrow is a mystery.
> But today is yours—to shape and relish.**

And today is your only chance to practice the previous twenty-six universal rules in this book.

Following are two examples of the way you can fully live today—smartly.

Movie Name: Today

Scene #2: *A Day with Dr. Smith*

Dr. Allen Smith is a fifty-year-old family physician.

On a typical weekday, he has a full calendar of appointments starting at 8 a.m. He has a habit of getting up at 6 a.m. *(Create Smart Habits, Rule 15)* so that he has enough time to shower, dress, have breakfast at a nearby coffee shop, and still arrive at his clinic on time.

By being efficient, he can do all this without being late, hurrying, or feeling stressed *(Avoid Psychological Inducers of Stress, Rule 10)*.

When he arrives at the café, he orders a decaf cappuccino. He gave up caffeinated drinks almost a year earlier after noticing that they compromised his quality of sleep *(Avoid Physical Inducers of Stress, Rule 10)*.

While waiting for his cappuccino, he reads the only newspaper he continues to have delivered after canceling his other subscriptions *(Eliminate Inessential Journal Subscriptions, Rule 6)*. He scans through it, checking the headlines and captions and reading the first and last paragraphs *(The Beginning-Captions-End Technique, Rule 6)*. If he wants more information, he reads the beginning of each paragraph and decides whether to skip it or go through *it (The Start-Skip Technique, Rule 6)*.

While sipping his cappuccino, he takes his daily supplements of vitamin D3, omega-3, turmeric, magnesium, and a multivitamin *(Staying Healthy, Rule 10)*.

And while waiting for his omelet, he checks his phone. He knows he only has about ten minutes to do so, but he is confident it won't take him any longer *(The Time-Windows Formula, Rule 6)*. The number of e-mails he receives has decreased significantly ever since he deleted two of his five e-mail accounts *(Eliminate Unnecessary E-mail Accounts, Rule 6)*. He also eliminated most promotional e-mails by unsubscribing, blocking some senders *(The Block/Unsubscribe Formula, Rule 6)*, or redirecting their messages to an otherwise inactive e-mail address *(Eliminate It, Rule 6)*.

Dr. Smith arrives at his office at 7:45 a.m., takes off his jacket, and puts on a crisp white coat *(Appearance Counts, Rule 25)*. The clinic today is very busy, but he likes it that way *(Keep Busy, Rule 10)*.

Although he doesn't spend too much time with any one patient, he makes a point of listening intently to every one of them *(Listen First, Talk Second, Rule 5)*. He also maintains eye contact while speaking with each patient *(Look Straight, Rule 4)*.

Around 11:30 a.m., he starts feeling hungry and a little tired, but he remembers that his lunch is just around the corner and looks forward to it *(Exciting Expectations, Rule 10)*.

At lunchtime, Dr. Smith follows his routine *(Create Smart Habits, Rule 15)* of walking for ten minutes *(Exercise, Rule 10)* to a cozy bistro, where he orders a soup and a small salad. He also orders a bottle of sparkling water to drink. He used to order a diet cola but stopped doing so years ago after he read about the possible adverse health effects of artificially sweetened beverages *(Good Nutrition, Rule 10)*.

While waiting for his lunch, he picks up his phone and spends a few minutes, for the second time today, checking his e-mails, texts, and voicemails *(The Time-Windows Formula, Rule 6)*. He answers some with a word or two *(The One-Minute Formula, Rule 6)* and ignores the rest. He leaves some of his personal unanswered phone calls for later, while he's driving home.

When he arrives back at his office around 1 p.m., his clinic manager, Carla, runs up to him. They have an emotional emergency in the waiting room. One of his patients, Elizabeth, is sobbing after she learned that the results of her breast MRI indicate cancer.

Dr. Smith is furious that Carla made a critical mistake in divulging the results of this MRI to his patient before he had a chance to speak with her face-to-face. His first instinct is to blast Carla and let her know how unprofessional and careless she was. However, he refrains from taking out his anger out on her.

Although Carla sometimes crosses the lines of propriety, she is nonetheless a very efficient and loyal assistant. Dr. Smith suspects that if he criticizes her too harshly, she may just quit. He simply can't afford to lose her *(Don't Gamble with What You Can't Afford to Lose, Rule 13)*. So, he decides to cool down and talk to her later. Meanwhile, he asks her to usher Elizabeth into his office ahead of the other patients.

Elizabeth enters the examination room crying. Dr. Smith is touched by her tears. He hesitates and isn't quite sure what to say, so he simply says nothing *(When You Don't Know What to Say, Say Nothing, Rule 12)*. He sits in front of her and just waits, looking kindly into her bloodshot eyes *(Look Straight, Rule 4)*.

A minute later, Elizabeth calms down and tells Dr. Smith in a trembling voice, "Doctor, I don't want to die."

Dr. Smith holds her hands and speaks slowly and quietly. "Calm down, Elizabeth. Your case is treatable." He notices a surprised look in her eyes. He continues, "The most probable outcome is that, once treated, you will live free of cancer" *(The Most Probable Scenario, Rule 9)*.

He adds, "Even if the disease comes back, it's not automatically a death sentence. Many patients with a recurrence or metastases beat the disease with today's state-of-the-art treatments" *(The Worst-Case Scenario, Rule 9)*.

Elizabeth, in a somewhat calmer state, interrupts him, "But why me, Dr. Smith? Why me? I have three sisters, and all of them are in perfect health."

Dr. Smith replies, "Despite the cancer, Elizabeth, you have a lot to be thankful for. Some patients discover the cancer at a much later stage, when an intervention could be too late" *(Remember What Could Have Happened, Rule 20)*. "Think of your blessings." *(Think of What You Have, Not What You Don't Have, Rule 20)*.

Elizabeth seems relieved and brightens up. She stands and hugs Dr. Smith, saying, "Thank you, Doctor—I feel much better already," and leaves with an appointment to see an oncologist.

The next patient enters the examination room with a long face and an unhappy expression. Dr. Smith asks him, "How are you, Mr. Cunningham?" The patient explodes,

"Not happy. My appointment was earlier than that crybaby who was just in here."

Dr. Smith is irritated by Mr. Cunningham's foul mood. For a second, he feels an urge to put his patient in his place and make him feel bad for his uninformed, rude comments, but he restrains himself *(Don't Get Even, Get Smart, Rule 23)*. He decides to wait and listen in silence instead *(Listen First, Talk Second, Rule 5; Silence Is Often Your Best Reply, Rule 12)*.

Mr. Cunningham continues talking, somewhat perplexed by Dr. Smith's silence. After he finishes airing his grievances, Dr. Smith finally says, "I understand how you feel, Mr. Cunningham, and I apologize" *(Start Every Argument with an Agreement, Rule 3)*.

Mr. Cunningham is speechless. He didn't expect Dr. Smith to agree with him.

Dr. Smith continues, "I had to see the other patient before you because of a serious emergency, but now I have all the time in the world for you, even if we make everyone else wait."

Mr. Cunningham smiles and replies in an almost apologetic voice, "That's okay, Doc. I didn't mean it."

The last patient in the clinic that day is a sixteen-year-old boy with a throat infection who comes for a follow-up visit. Dr. Smith expects the results of the culture taken a week ago to be in the patient's chart, but it isn't. He thinks, *What am I going to do with my receptionist, Maria? She doesn't get it.* He has told her a hundred times to enter the test results in the corresponding patients' charts weekly, but she keeps forgetting to do so *(People Don't Change, Rule 18)*.

In spite of that, Dr. Smith likes Maria as a person. His patients love her friendly approach and her smiling face. He figures that if he gives her the same admonition he always gives her, it still won't work *(Seed A Will Give You Plant A, Every Single Time, Rule 19)*.

So, after seeing his last patient, Dr. Smith asks Maria to meet with him. He tells her that he has decided to change the system for handling all incoming test results *(If You Want a Different Reaction, Try a Different Action, Rule 19)*. He explains that instead of waiting until the end of the week to enter the test results into each patient's chart, the new office policy will be to place them immediately in the corresponding file the day they are received.

Maria is more than happy to oblige, and leaves the room relieved that she didn't have to justify her absentmindedness.

Dr. Smith then calls Carla, his clinic manager, into his office. He starts by saying, "Carla, you're an excellent office manager. You're efficient and loyal" *(Start Every Criticism with a Compliment, Rule 3)*. Carla is flattered.

Dr. Smith continues, "Sometimes, however, you're too eager to help, and you end up giving too much information to patients before I can see them. In the future, I would appreciate it if you clear any such disclosures of information with me first."

Carla, having been complimented initially, doesn't feel humiliated by the subsequent criticism. She utters a brief "Sorry" and promises to follow the new directive.

As he watches her leave the room, Dr. Smith reflects on the fact that Carla is indispensable to him. But Carla is a human being. She can fall sick or change her mind about working with him. Her husband, a banker, travels often for work and was thinking a year ago of changing locations. If he does, Carla would surely resign to be with her husband, even though she loves her job.

Suddenly, Dr. Smith feels vulnerable. He decides that he should start grooming Maria for some of Carla's office management duties, *(Always Have a Safety Net, Just in Case, Rule 24)*. He even thinks it may be a good idea to hire a part-time assistant for a few hours a week in case either Carla or Maria can't make it to work.

On his way home, Dr. Smith returns one of his phone calls. It's from his friend John. He likes John and makes an effort to stay in touch with him *(Happiness Is Feeling Connected, Rule 10)*. After enjoying a pleasant ten-minute chat, Dr. Smith feels he shouldn't allow the conversation to stretch any further, lest it become boring and reflect negatively on him. So, he finds an excuse to terminate the call *(Don't Dilute Your Presence with Too Much Presence, Rule 7)*.

After he arrives home, Dr. Smith changes into casual clothes and has a nice supper. After that, he enjoys the fifteen-minute time slot he's reserved for relaxation *(Create Smart Habits, Rule 15)*. He really looks forward to this precious respite *(Exciting Expectations, Rule 10)*. Depending on his mood, he reads, watches TV, or takes a short nap. Fifteen minutes may not seem like much, but to Dr. Smith it's a feasible time frame that's rewarding and practical *(Do It Now, Perfect It Later, Rule 1)*. And he made a deal with his wife that she won't interrupt him during this scheduled brief relaxation *(Involve Another Person with Your Habit, Rule 15)*.

As he gets ready for bed, Dr. Smith feels fulfilled. After only five minutes of his usual bedtime reading *(Do It Now, Perfect It Later, Rule 1; Create Smart Habits, Rule 15)*, he falls soundly asleep.

Movie Name: Today

Scene #3: *A Day with Anna*

Anna is a thirty-two-year-old surgical resident who graduated from the same medical school as Dr. Smith, albeit many years later. Instead of practicing family medicine, she opted to specialize in surgery and is now in her fourth year of surgical residency.

Anna finds her schedule overwhelming. She attempts to balance the demands of her career with marriage and motherhood (she and her husband have an eight-year-old son), but it's almost impossible.

Every day, she is up at 5 a.m. to make rounds at the hospital by 6:30 a.m. She then races to the operating room at 7:30 a.m. From then on, it's a nonstop marathon that only finishes around 6 p.m.

And that's not all. After this full and demanding day of work, if she is on call, she has to be available to run back to the hospital for emergencies. And no matter what happens during the night, she is still expected to show up promptly the next day for rounds at 6:30 a.m., as if nothing had happened.

In addition to all this, she is supposed to find time to study and prepare for her final exams.

It's no wonder Anna is sleep-deprived and chronically exhausted. As well, she feels guilty because she can't spend more time with her son, and because her relationship with her husband is suffering.

Today, as she returns home from work, she is tired, depressed, and feeling desperate. She decides that this can't go on any longer. All day long, she has been thinking about what to do, feeling as if she is on the verge of a nervous breakdown.

As a last resort, she sits down, takes out a piece of paper, and decides to analyze her situation *(Put Your Problems on Paper, Rule 8)*.

Her first problem is lack of time.

As she enumerates, on paper, all her daily duties, she chooses to eliminate some time-consuming but not crucial tasks *(Eliminate It, Rule 6)*. As well, she decides to hire a cleaning lady for the apartment *(Delegate It, Rule 6)*. And instead of cooking daily, she will ask her mother to prepare some meals for her *(Ask Once for What You Want, Rule 2)*. She immediately picks up the phone and calls her mother *(Do It Now, Perfect It Later, Rule 1)*, who happily agrees to cook four meals a week and even deliver them.

Furthermore, Anna decides to silence her social media *(the Social Media/Apps Formula, Rule 6)* and ignore all e-mails except for those sent to her university account *(Eliminate Unnecessary E-mail Accounts, Rule 6)*.

Another time waster is online shopping.

Anna often spends hours looking at merchandise she doesn't need just so she can feel good about the supposedly great deals she's offered, which often end up being costly blunders *(Flip the Freebie and Look for the Hidden Price Tag, Rule 17)*. The time she spends on comparison shopping negates the savings. So, she decides that she will only buy products she genuinely needs from now on, will order them online in seconds, and will choose reasonably priced items from reputable, trusted sources *(When You Trust Others, Be Careful, Rule 22)*.

Another issue is her studying schedule.

The prospect of sitting down at her desk for two to three hours at a time is so unenticing that she ends up finding excuses to skip the sessions altogether. Today, after comparing her options on paper *(Put Your Problems on Paper, Rule 8)*, she comes up with a new idea. She designs a fixed schedule for Saturdays and Sundays, devoting four hours to studying each day *(Create Smart Habits, Rule 15)*, but stopping for a fifteen-minute break after each hour *(Exciting Expectations, Rule 10)*.

In addition, she decides that instead of tackling an intimidating thousand-page textbook and struggling to absorb all those scientific details, she will start with a much smaller book that summarizes the contents. By doing so, she can concentrate on the essential information for now *(Do It Now, Perfect It Later, Rule 1)* and absorb as much material as she can in the time that she has. Once she gets a good grasp of the basic information, she will then be able to more easily tackle the detailed textbook.

Anna feels relieved that she has come up with these smart strategies to reduce her stress and solve her time management dilemma, as well as her shopping and studying issues. However, she is not ready to celebrate yet.

She goes back to her paper to solve her remaining challenges.

Lately, she has been feeling bad about her roles as a wife and mother *(That Sinking Feeling Inside Means Stop, Rule 14)*. Anna had a marriage based on love, and the first few years were wonderful, especially after she gave birth to her son. Lately, though, her relationship with her husband has soured. Feeling pushed away by her incessant busyness, he has become resentful and distant. Anna was so upset at him for not understanding her time issues that she even fleetingly considered filing for divorce. But she thought she would be taking a dangerous risk with her married life and was worried that she might regret it later *(Don't Gamble with What You Can't Afford to Lose, Rule 13)*. She hesitated, so she waited *(When You Don't Know What to Do, Do Nothing, Rule 11)*.

Today, the more she thinks about her marriage and how much she loves her husband, the more motivated she becomes to save their relationship. She appreciates the fact that her husband, even when he's irritated with her, has never betrayed her trust and always keeps his word *(When Other People Trust You, Be Honorable, Rule 22)*. She makes the decision to work on her marriage and is confident that she will succeed *(Never Give In or Give Up, Rule 26)*. So, she again sits down to evaluate what's happening and to find solutions.

Taking a deep breath, with her paper in front of her, she writes down all the possible reasons for her failing marriage *(Put Your Problems on Paper, Rule 8)*. To her surprise, she discovers that she is the one to blame for most of them. She recognizes that she is always talking about her work or focusing on their son, putting her husband last. And she realizes that the reason that her husband seems distant may be because she neglects her appearance and always offers excuses about being tired and busy. Worse, she admits that she constantly interrupts her husband to check her phone or talk to her son, which only makes him more irritated.

Anna now knows that she can't put the blame on her husband anymore and that improving her marriage is her own responsibility *(The Ball Is in Your Court, the Change Has to Come from You, Rule 19)*. It's up to her to learn from her mistakes *(Learn from Your Mistakes and Other People's Mistakes, Rule 21)*. She comes to the conclusion that changing her husband's attitude toward her depends on her commitment to changing her own behavior *(If You Want a Different Reaction, Try a Different Action, Rule 19)*.

She decides that, from now on, she will give her husband her undivided attention when he wants to talk to her *(Unitask, Don't Multitask, Rule 16)*. She also makes the decision to occasionally hire her neighbor's young daughter as a babysitter so that she can have more leisure time with her husband *(Delegate It, Rule 6)*.

Then, she picks up the phone and books a candlelit dinner for two for the coming weekend. She intends, during that evening, to review with her husband her new resolutions. She will explain her plans to him and ask for his support in implementing them *(Involve Another Person in Your Habit, Rule 15)*. She is almost sure that her husband will appreciate her initiative and eagerness for their relationship to be revived.

Anna looks once again at her written notes and contemplates her new decisions. She experiences, for the first time in a long time, a reassuring feeling of satisfaction and hope.

She gets up energized and finally feels like celebrating. She suggests, to the astonishment of her husband and son, that they all go out for ice cream. Both father and son are pleasantly surprised and concur wholeheartedly.

Movie Name: Today

Scene #4: *The End*

So, as you have seen in the *todays* of Dr. Smith and Anna, lots of rewarding successes can be achieved in just one day—TODAY.

Especially when you apply The Universal Rules of Life!

Movie Name: Today

Scene #5: *The Sequel*

Now, what's next?

In all likelihood, you have enjoyed this book and may have already started applying some of its rules while reading it. And you're probably planning on using many of these rules in the future.

The problem, however, is that, as I said before, *lasting impressions are far from guaranteed.* Our memory for self-improvement is short-lived. We forget our learned lessons easily. And we tend to relapse sooner or later.

But is there any way for you to easily recall, remember, and apply the Universal Rules of Life . . . for the rest of your life?

Yes, there is.

I've included a short, crisp, and easy-to-read recapitulation of the rules in an elegant appendix at the end of this book, titled "The Universal Rules of Life—In A Pearl Shell." You should review this rules synopsis yearly, ideally on the morning following the passing New Year's celebration.

So:

> **Every January 1, take just**
> **5 minutes of your time**
> **to cruise through the "Universal Rules of Life" summary.**

This *"Do it now, perfect it later"* action will only take the most rewarding five minutes you spend every year and will repeatedly refresh your memory of the 27 highly valuable "Universal Rules of Life."

Your life depends on it!

RULE 27

in a Pearl Shell

TODAY Is All You've Got!
*It's the Only Live Movie
You Can Act In, Edit, and Enjoy;
Yesterday's Movie Can't Be Rewound,
and Tomorrow's Movie Isn't Out Yet!*

- *Yesterday Is History*
- *Tomorrow Is a Mystery*
- *But TODAY Is Yours, to Shape and Enjoy*
  It's All You've Got
  and It's Your Only Chance to Practice the 27 *Universal Rules of Life!*
- Every January 1, Take Just *5 Minutes of Your Time* to Cruise Through the "Universal Rules of Life" Summary
  Your Life Depends On It!

ACKNOWLEDGMENTS

I would like to express my very special thanks to Glenn Plaskin, the highly talented international bestselling author, for his much-appreciated input, his exceptionally sophisticated feedback, and his invaluable advice during the writing process.

Most important, I am especially grateful to my publisher, Jonathan Merkh, president of Forefront Books, for being ever-present for opinion and advice, for his total persistence and insistence on ensuring the highest quality and good taste for this book, and for his unwavering commitment to its success.

Big thanks are due to my wife, Stephanie, for the time spent reading and evaluating the different versions of the book, and for her precious opinions during its conception.

My gratitude goes to the following colleagues, friends and family members for their very appreciated help and inspiring suggestions: Dr. Christine Bishara, Dr. Kristina Zakhary, Mr. Sam Joseph, Miss Cynthia Lecompte, Mr. Jason Rahal, Dr. Sam Fanous, Dr. Amanda Fanous, Dr. Emad Fahmy, Mr. Ramy Kirollos, Mrs. Karen Fahmy, Mrs. Manal Fahmy, Dr. Kamal Ibrahim, Mr. Samih Fanous, Dr. Michael Nissenbaum, Mr. Kamal Mekhael, Mr. Joseph Mekhael, and Mr. Mathieu Beaudriault.

Special thanks are due to editors Billie Brownell for her valuable suggestions, Barbara Clark for her thoughtful contribution to the manuscript, Rick Wolff for his clever editorial tips and Jennifer Gingerich, editorial director, for putting everything together .

Big thanks are due to Bruce Gore for the exquisite cover design, and to Bill Kersey for the highly skillful interior design.

DISCLAIMER

The names and identifying details of the persons mentioned in the true stories of this book have been changed. This book is addressed to a general audience and is not indented as a substitute for relevant individual advice, whether personal or medical.

THE UNIVERSAL RULES of LIFE

In a Pearl Shell

5-MINUTE SUMMARY

RULE 1

Do It Now, Perfect It Later
Stop the "I Will" Habit

- *We Fail Because We Never Begin*
- Do Like Newton's Apple:
  Start Moving . . . and the Rest Will Follow
- *Surrender Perfectionism*
- *Just Do Something, Anything—But Do It Now*
  And Later, You Can Perfect It

RULE 2

Ask Once for What You Want
And You Will Get It 50% of the Time

- *Don't Be the Doormat!*
- *Ask Once for What You Want*
- Occasionally, *Ask Twice* if Courageous, and a *Thousand Times* if Desperate
- *You Really Have Nothing to Lose!*

RULE 3

Start Every Criticism with a Compliment, and Every Argument with an Agreement
How to Criticize and Argue, Yet Remain Liked and Respected

Criticizing
- *A Criticism Is Forever*
- We Are Fast to Criticize, and Slow to Praise

- *Start Every Criticism with a Compliment*
- Be *Generous* with Your Compliments, *Brief* with Your Criticisms
- *In Every Rough, There Is a Diamond!*
  Look for the *Diamond in the Rough*

Arguing
- *Don't Start an Argument by...Arguing!*
- *Start Every Argument with an Agreement*
- Let Your Opponent *Score First*, So That You Can *Score Second*
- If You Can't Agree on Something, Just Say,
  "I Understand What You Mean"

RULE 4

Stand Straight, Look Straight
*How Your Posture and Gaze Can Create a Commanding
Presence...Before You Even Utter a Word*

- *Slumped Posture and Poor Eye Focus*—Are the *King and Queen*
  of Bad First Impressions
- *Confident Posture and Focused Gaze*—Are the Recipe for a
  Commanding First Impression
- You Have Got *One-Tenth-of-a-Second Chance...*
  And You Will Never Get *a Second* Chance!

RULE 5

Listen First, Talk Second
How to Mesmerize Anyone You Talk To

- *Listening Is a Magnetic Force*
- Start by *Listening* before You Start *Talking*
- When You Listen, *Listen with Your Ears and Eyes*
  Hear What's Not Said, and *See* What's Not Seen!
- And Before You Talk, *Wait—Like the Rest of the Orchestra!*

RULE 6

Eliminate It, Delegate It, or Shrink It!
*The Three Time-Management Secrets of Doing ...
What You Don't Have Time to Do*

The First Secret of Time Management
The best way to do something *that doesn't need to be done ...
is not to do it at all!*
In other words: ***Eliminate it.***
- *Implement the Seven Smart Formulas*
    1 - Three Time-Windows; 2 - A Minute Is a Long Time;
    3 - Silenced Notifications; 4 - It's a Phone Ring, Not a
    Command; 5 - Block Unwanted Callers and E-mails;
    6 - Limit Social Media and Apps; 7 - Stop CC and Reply All
- *Eliminate Unnecessary E-mail Accounts*
- *Restrict TV Viewership and Non-essential Journal Subscriptions*

The Second Secret of Time Management
The best way to do something *you don't have to do personally ...
is to let someone else do it for you!*
In other words: ***Delegate it.***
- *Teach and Delegate, then Check and Re-Check*

The Third Secret of Time Management
If you can't eliminate it and can't delegate it ...
then at least ***shrink it!***
- *Shrink Any Task* —by Trimming Its *Unnecessary* Parts
- *Shrink the Time You Give Yourself to Do Something* —and You
    Will End Up Doing It *on Time!*
- *Shrink Reading and Writing*—"Beginning-Captions-End,"
    "Start-Skip Paragraph," and "Voice Activation" Techniques

Then
You Will Have the Time *to Do ...*
What You Really Want *to Do!*

RULE 7

Don't Dilute Your Presence . . . with Too Much Presence
The First Spoon of Honey Is a Delight, the Tenth Is a Turnoff!

- It's *Supply and Demand*
- *Don't Cheapen Your Presence* by Offering Too Much of It
- Know *When to Leave the Stage*, and *When Enough Is Enough*
- *Don't Call* Too Often, *Talk* for Too Long, or *Overstay* Your Welcome
- And Learn from the Aluminum Story: *Be Hard to Get!*

RULE 8

Put Your Problems on Paper
How to Solve Any Problem in Less Than 5 Minutes

- Don't Burden Your Brain with Trivia
- *Stop the "Whirlpool Whirling"*
- When Facing a Problem, *Use the "5-Minute" Formula—on Paper*
- Keep Your Trip on Track ✓, with Destination Known
- *Make Your Priority List*
- Keep *Notepads* Handy

RULE 9

What's the Worst-Case Scenario?
And What's the Most Probable One?

Just Follow the Weather!

For a Little Storm, Ask Yourself:
- *Will I Remember It 6 Months Down the Road?*
  It's *Useless* to Worry About *Useless* Things

For a Big Storm, Ask Yourself:
- *What's the Worst-Case Scenario?*
  Often, It *Isn't the End of the World,* and It's *Improbable*
- *What's the Most Probable Scenario?*
  Often, It *Isn't that Bad,* and It's *Most Likely* to Happen

RULE 10

Your #1 Goal in Life Is Happiness
How to Implement the Four Indispensable Secrets of Living Happily

THE FIRST SECRET OF HAPPINESS
Working and Keeping Busy
Happiness Isn't *Owning* Things . . . but *Doing* Things!
- No Object—Once Obtained—Can Keep You Perpetually Entertained
- What's Important Isn't Owning Things, But Doing Things
- You Need Something to Get Up for Every Morning
- Keep Working, Keep Busy
- The Harder You Work During the Week, the More You Enjoy Your Weekend!

THE SECOND SECRET OF HAPPINESS
Having Exciting Expectations
Happiness Is the Yellow Brick Road to the Exciting
Goal . . . That Ends Once You Reach That *Goal*!
- Thrilling Expectations Give You Something to Look for in the Future
- Like Dorothy's Enchanted Trip, Happiness Is the Yellow Brick Road to the Exciting Goal
  But Once You Reach That Goal . . . You Need to Find Another Exciting One
- Your Life Should Be a Succession of Exciting Goals

THE THIRD SECRET OF HAPPINESS
Staying Healthy
The Crucial Steps for *Prevention and Early Detection*
of Cancer, Heart Disease, Diabetes, and Alzheimer's Disease
- If You're Sick, It's Difficult to Be Happy
- Stay Healthy Both Physically and Psychologically
- The Best Cure of All Is Prevention and Early Detection
- Check with Your Physician First, and With Your Common Sense Second

THE FOURTH SECRET OF HAPPINESS
Having a *Family and Friends* Network
Happiness Is *Feeling Connected*
- Loneliness Is a Silent Killer
- We Crave to Belong and Be Loved
- Family and Friends Want One Thing from You: Your Time
  Block Off 5 Minutes Daily for Them

RULE 11

When You Don't Know What to Do ...
Do Nothing!
Time Will Often Reveal the Solution

- When Hesitating Between Multiple Options,
  Do Nothing—and Wait
- Sooner or Later, *Time Will Upgrade the Right Option*
- And Don't Allow Yourself to Be Rushed
  You Owe No Actions ... to Anyone

RULE 12

When You Don't Know What to Say ...
Say Nothing!
Silence Is Often Your Best Reply

- *Silence Is Awkward*
- If You're Struggling to Respond, *Dive into Silence*
- *You Owe No Answers ... to Anyone*
- If Pressed, Say, *"I'll Think About It."*
- *If You Don't Feel Like Smiling, Don't*
- And Let the *Taboo Trio* Pass: *Sex, Religion, and Politics*
- *There Is Power in Saying Nothing*

RULE 13

Don't Gamble with What
You Can't Afford to Lose
Luck Is Fickle

- *Don't Trust Your Luck or Your Intelligence*
  Never Gamble with an Asset Crucial to You

- In the Casino of Life, as in the Neighborhood Casino: *The House Always Wins—Not You!*
- *In Gambling, Sooner or Later, Lightning Will Strike!* The Dice Will Deliver the *Least Expected Numbers,* and Then . . . You Lose and Are Lost!

RULE 14

That Sinking Feeling Inside Means—STOP
That Four-Million-Year-Old Alarm System Within Us

- When You Feel a *Knot in Your Stomach,* It's Telling You: *STOP*—and Watch Out for Trouble
- You Need to *Think* Why You Felt That Way: When You Start *Sinking* . . . Start *Thinking!*

RULE 15

Create Smart Habits That Simplify Your Life
The Magic of Automated Living

- We Are *Creatures of Habit*
- Only an *Effortless Good Habit* Can Overcome an *Effortless Bad One*
  "One Nail In, One Nail Out"
- *To Create Smart Habits, Implement the Three Musketeers Conditions:*
  - 1 - *Offer a Reasonable Deal to Your Brain:* Your Brain Will Reject Any Rotten Deal
  - 2 - *Repeat the New Habit for a Month:* Repetition Works, Repetition Works
  - 3 - *Get A Buddy System:* Another Party Gets into the Habit . . . of Being Part of Your Habit!
- Then, Relax and Enjoy *The Magic of Automated Living*

RULE 16

Unitask,
Don't Multitask
How to Be Laser-Focused and Highly Productive,
Yet Totally Stress-Free and in the Moment

- *Don't Be a Circus Acrobat*, Juggling Pins in the Air, Spinning Here, There, and Everywhere
- *Don't Try to Have It All, Do It All, All at Once*
  You Will Be *Very Busy* . . . Doing *Very Little*
- *Unitask* as Often as Possible, *Multitask* as Seldom as Possible
- And Let Your *Eyes* Choose the Unitask:
  Where Your Eyes Go . . . You Go!

RULE 17

Flip the Freebie . . .
and Look for the Hidden Price Tag!
Nothing Is Free

- *For Every Freebie*, Something of an *Equal or Higher Value* Will Be Either:
  Taken Away from You . . . or *Given Away* by You!
  Almost Always!
- *When It Sounds Too Good to Be True . . . It Is!*

RULE 18

People Don't Change
And Even If They Do Change, They Often Change Back!

- *Biology Wins Over Environment*
  Personalities Are Encrypted into Our Genes
- *People Don't Change Easily*
  And Even If They *Do Change*, They Tend to *Revert Back*
- *Try Just Once or Twice to Change Them*
  Then, *Quit Squeezing the Stone*, and Follow Rule 19!

RULE 19

Seed A
Will Give You
Plant A . . .
Every Single Time
If You Want a Different Plant, Try a Different Seed!

- Remember Einstein's Theory of Insanity:
  Repetition Doesn't Work
- Don't Do the *Same Thing* Over and Over Again, While
  Expecting a *Different Result*
- If You Plant *Seed A*, It Will Grow into *Plant A . . .*
  Every Single Time
- And If You Take *Action A*, It Will Elicit *Reaction A . . .*
  Every Single Time
- *The Change Has to Come from YOU*
  By Changing Your Action, You Change People's Reaction
- *The Ball Is in Your Court!*

RULE 20

Think of What You Have,
Not What You Don't Have
And Think of What Other People DON'T Have,
Not What They DO Have

- *Stop Comparing and Despairing*
  Count Your Blessings, Not Your Sorrows
- Remember What You *Have*, Not What You *Don't Have*
- Don't Complain About What You're Missing, Because:
  You Will Never Find Out . . . What the Others Are Missing
  People Air Their Good News, But Hide Their Not-So-
  Flattering Sides
- *Your Cravings Will Never Be Quenched*
  Whatever You Achieve in Life, There Will Always Be Someone
  Else Who Will Beat You at It!
- Make Your *Gratitude List,* Today
- *Remember the Misfortunes That Could Have Happened to*
  You . . . But Didn't
  Then, Be Grateful and Celebrate

RULE 21

Learning from Your Own Mistakes Is Good,

Learning from Other People's Mistakes Is Even Better!
It's Smarter to Use a Scientifically Tested Medicine,
Than to Try an Experimental One

- Learning from Your *Own Mistakes* Is Good—*but Painful*
- Learning from the *Mistakes of Others* Is Even Better—*and*
  Painless
- *Write Every Mistake in Your Notebook,* and Review Regularly

RULE 22

When Other People Trust You, Be Honorable,

But When You Trust Other People, Be Careful!
Trust Is Tricky

When *Other People* Trust You
- *If Your Instincts Tell You to Run . . . RUN!*
  Simply Say, *"I'll Think About It"*

But When *You* Trust Others
- *Your Yes Is Your Oath,* and *Your Word Is Your Bond*
- *Never Promise* Unless You Can Deliver, and *Always Deliver*
  Whatever You Promise
- *Don't Be an Iscariot*—Never Betray the People Who Trust You
- *Faith Is Holy, Trust Is Not*
- *Never Ever Give Trust a Blank Check*
  And Make Sure You *Cut the Cards!*
- *Trust Is Time-Based*
- *Your Trust Elevator Should Take Its Time—Big Time*
  It Should Never Reach Floor 10, the Penthouse!
- Beware of the *Triple Trust Traps:*
  Money, Love, and Health

RULE 23

Don't Get Even, Get Smart!
Do What's Best for You, Not What's Best for Your Anger

- *Seeking Revenge Is Like Swallowing a Poison . . .* and Expecting the
  Other Person to Die from It!
- *The Flames of Rage Consume You First,* Before Reaching
  Your Enemy

- *Focus on What's Good for You—Not on What's Bad for Your Enemy*
- *What Happens to Your Aggressor* Is of Negligible Importance to You—However Major It Is,
  But What Happens to You Is of Major Importance to You— However Negligible It Is!
- *Look Out for #1—YOU*
- *Don't Get Even—Get Even Better!*
  Use Your *Brain*, Not Your *Emotions*

RULE 24

Always Have a Safety Net—Just in Case!
The Wisdom of Plan B

- *Don't Put All Your Eggs in One Basket*
  In Life, Things May Not Turn Out the Way You Expect
- *When Something Is a Big Deal for You,* Always Have a Safety Net—*Just in Case!*
- *You're in Great Shape* When You Have a Plan B,
  And in *Great Trouble* When You Don't Have One

RULE 25

Appearance Counts
For You, and Everyone, and Everything Around You

- *What You Look Like—Is How the World Perceives You*
- *Your Looks Affect Everyone Else*—Just as Everyone Else's Looks Affect You
- *People Are Judged by Their Looks*—Just as a Book Is Judged by Its Cover
- Even *Your Surroundings* Represent You
- Make the Effort to *Look Your Best* Every Single Day
- *Enhanced Looks . . . Enhance Lives*

- *What Comes First . . . Ranks First*
  Looks May Be More Crucial than Personality—When We Meet
  Someone for the First Time
- What We See as Beautiful—Is What Nature Wants Us to See as
  Beautiful!
- *Beauty Is a Blessing, But It Comes with a Curse Called "Aging"!*
- *With Age, Our Bodies May Be Relatively Young, While Our
  Faces Aren't*
  It's a Disconnect Between *Our Outside vs. Our Inside*
- And, by the Way, *How's Your "Morning Mirror" Test?!*

RULE 26

If You Feel Unbeatable, You Are
Only YOU Can Lower Your Head!

- *Good Luck Is Never Forever*
- Our Well-being Is Mostly Controlled from . . .
  within Our Heads!
- When Faced with Past Blows, *Blow Them Up!*
  Make Them *Gone and Forgotten*
- When Faced with Current Blows, *Be A Churchill!*
  Never, Never, Never *Give In* or *Give Up*
- *Walk and Behave Like a Loser . . .* and the Whole World Will
  Take Your Word for It!
  When You're *Down,* and When You Walk Bent *Down,* with
  Your Head *Down*—People Will Look *Down* on You!
- *Walk and Behave Like a Winner . . .* and Others Will Treat
  You as One. They May Doubt You at First, but Will End Up
  Doubting Themselves!

RULE 27

TODAY Is All You've Got
*It's the Only Live Movie
You Can Act In, Edit, and Enjoy;
Yesterday's Movie Can't Be Rewound,
and Tomorrow's Movie Isn't Out Yet!*

- *Yesterday Is History*
- *Tomorrow Is a Mystery*
- *But TODAY Is Yours, to Shape and Enjoy*
  It's All You've Got
  and It's Your Only Chance to Practice the 27 *Universal Rules of Life!*
- Every January 1, Take Just *5 Minutes of Your Time* to Cruise Through the Universal Rules' 5-Minute Summary
  Your Life Depends On It!